A BRIEF HISTORY OF THE VILLAGE OF FERRUM, VIRGINIA

1892 - 2019

KARL L. EDWARDS

Front Cover Photo: The Ferrum Railroad Station circa 1920.
Courtesy of the Blue Ridge Institute.

Back Cover Photo: J.K. Hurt and Company Building circa 1908.
Courtesy of the Blue Ridge Institute.

Library of Congress Cataloging-In-Publication Data

Pending

Library of Congress Control Number:2019916630

ISBN: 9781698543604

www.blueridgeinstitute.org

Blue Ridge Institute & Museum

Ferrum College

P. O. Box 1000

Ferrum, Virginia 24088

Proceeds from the sale of this book go to the

Blue Ridge Institute & Museum

Physical Location

20 Museum Drive

Ferrum, Virginia 24088

(540) 365 - 4412 - bri@ferrum.edu

Contents

Foreword

There is no one better suited to write a comprehensive historical account of the Village of Ferrum than Karl Edwards. My first encounter with Karl was as his British Literature student in the 12th grade at Franklin County High School in Rocky Mount. Karl had a presence in the class unlike any other teacher. It was evident that he knew the subject matter and that we were going to be educated. As Director of the Institute, I once again saw Karl while he was using the Blue Ridge Heritage Archives for research. Nothing had changed in the passing years. Karl, who is a native of Ferrum, had a goal of writing a book about the village, and he has produced a text filled with the most accurately detailed events, anecdotes, and rare photographs to be found. The book will serve as the ideal reference on Ferrum and has been devotedly prepared by the person who was the one to write it.

Bethany Worley, Director

Blue Ridge Institute and Museum of Ferrum College

Acknowledgements

It is with sincere appreciation that I acknowledge the help of the following people who graciously answered my questions, suggested other folks to contact, contributed pictures, newspaper clippings, as well as other materials, aided my research and offered their encouragement:

K. Edward Goode; Dorothy Hodges and the staff of the Franklin County Public Library; Roddy Moore, Bethany Worley, Vaughn Webb, Patricia H. Carter, Jenny Rorrer, Rebecca Austin, Krystal Davis, and others on the staff of the Blue Ridge Institute; Ken Miller, Harry Bundy, Jim Blackstock of the Norfolk and Western Historical Society; the staff of the Virginia Room of the Roanoke City Public Library; Dr. J. Francis Amos; Anne Carter Lee Gravely; Ruby Woods Worley; Irene Hatcher Burnett; Linda Stanley, Doris Eames, Ilene Lavinder, Frances Dillon of the Franklin County Historical Society; Dorothy Cundiff; Peggy Barker, Cheryl Hundley, Brandi Porter of the Ferrum College Library; Teresa Brown and the staff of Clerk of the Circuit Court of Franklin County; Beverly Merritt; Morris Stephenson, Kitty Martin; Linda Peters Edwards, Mabel Hale Webb; Doris Ann Radford; Jean Ingram Meador; Larry Bowling; David Clements; C.B. Nolen. Jr.; Carolyn Nolen Peck; Claude B. Nolen, III; Lane Hash; Gail Sigmon; Peggy and Lloyd Edwards; James Gearhart; Colonel James Stanley; Dexter Mullins; Hugh and Shirley Young Green; Cecil Young; Geneva Richardson Le Monde;

Nancy Wilson Long; Edward and Doris Montgomery; Sybil Brammer Winesett; Shirley Dodson Wright; Joyce Dodson Scott; Debra Buckner Scott; Lucille Thompson Woody; Leo and Geraldine Nolen Scott, Wanda Frith Fischbach, Elvie Kesler Wright; Becky Worley Turner, Dr. Greg Turner; J.B. Edwards, Jr.; Roger Edwards; Randell Edwards; Rev. Mary S. White; Robert Journell; Phyllis Woods Holley; Margie Chaney Angle; Doug Minnix; Wayne and Susan Dudley; Dillard Thompson; Dr. Charles Thompson; Bruce and Doris Martin; Roy and Hazel Hale; Harold Ingram; Steve Thomas; Madelyn Hall; Debra Peters Huff; Kathy Radford Zernhelt; Paul and Heddy Cooper Radford; Belle Nolen Cooper; Cooper Woolson; Donald and Vera Shively; Raymond Keys; John Speidel; James G. Keith, III; James Shively; Tilden Riddle; Melissa Prillaman; James Nagy; Lynn Maxey; Harold Mullins; Lisa Whitlock; Larry Meadors; Josh Gibson; L. D. Arrington; Charlene Peters Robinson; Carolyn Hale Bruce; David Newcombe; Peggy Smith; Evelyn Patterson Dowdy; Mary Jane Lynch; Glenda Scott Thompson; Marsha Stanley Fay; Walter H. Green; Charles W. (Butch) Blankenship; John Luther Smith; Lester Shively; Donnie Scott; Terry Dameron; Justin Woodrow; Virgil H. Goode, Jr.; Mary Stoudt; Christian Haley.

I would also like to thank the following people for reviewing all or parts of the manuscript and making suggestions: Dr. J. Francis Amos, Linda Stanley, Roddy Moore, Bethany Worley, K. Edward Goode, and Ariel Hundley.

I especially want to recognize Ariel Hundley, Curator of the Blue Ridge Institue & Museum, for her many hours of layout and editorial assistance. Her knowledge and computer skills have been invaluable in the completion of this project.

This pen and ink drawing depicts Saint James United Methodist Church, the oldest standing structure in the Village of Ferrum, constructed in 1896-1897. (S.J.U.M.C. Stationery - Undated)

Chapter 1
The Eighteenth Century and Before

Before the arrival of the first permanent English settlers in Virginia in 1607, the hills and valleys of what is today southwestern Franklin County had been home to small bands of Native Americans for thousands of years. Members of the Tutelo and Saponi tribes hunted, fished, gathered nuts, berries, roots, and leaves; they also would have planted corn, pumpkins and squash in the area. Remains of native villages have been found on Otter Creek in southwestern Franklin County and on Town Creek just south of the county line in Henry County. Other village sites have been located on the Smith River near the mouth of Nicholas Creek (now under Philpott Lake) and on the Pigg River near the mouth of Turners Creek (Salmon 11). Scattered pottery sherds, stone projectile points and cutting tools in their thousands and a few V-shaped fish traps on the Pigg and Blackwater Rivers bear witness to these original inhabitants.

Prior to the coming of the settlers, generations of Tutelo and Saponi endured periodic raids by warriors from the northern Iroquois nation who followed animal trails southward along what would come to be called the Great Warriors Trace or Path. Because the Warriors Path came directly through modern Franklin County the weak bands of Native Americans living here were extremely vulnerable to these raiding parties. Ironically, this internecine tribal warfare was most probably responsible for the local natives having been either destroyed or dispersed before the settlers' arrival in the eighteenth century. In fact, Thomas Batts and Robert Fallom, early English explorers, encountered no natives while passing through this area in 1671 (Salmon 13). In his *Genesis of a Virginia Frontier: The Origins of Franklin County, Virginia, 1740-1785*, Keister Greer captured the poignancy of the disappearance of the Native Americans from this land they had occupied for generations:

> The redman seems to have disappeared all at once; one moment he was there, the next he had gone, and we read of him no more. It is only when the plow strikes a flint axe, or turns up an

Figure 1.   These Stone Age Native American artifacts including a cutting tool, spear points, and arrowheads were found near Ferrum and range in age from approximately 2,000 to 10,000 years old. (From author's collection)

arrowhead, that we think of those hundreds of years when from Chestnut Mountain to Maggoty Gap, the Indian surveyed the land that was his. (11)

It would be another seventy years before men like John Pigg, for whom the Pigg River is named, would arrive to lay the first claims to lands in what is now Pittsylvannia County near southeastern Franklin County (Salmon 22). By about 1745 Robert Hill had settled on land by the river that bore Pigg's name; John, Mark, and Stephen Cole secured land patents on the Blackwater River and gave their name to its tributary Coles Creek around 1756; the Jones brothers Robert and Thomas were granted patents on the upper Pigg River and Turner's Creek in 1755 and 1760; in the 1750's Robert Pusey secured lands on Otter Creek and Blackwater River adjoining the lands of Richard Randolph (Greer, *Genesis* 13-30).

In 1740 the Virginia House of Burgesses offered tax exemptions in an attempt to encourage settlement of the western frontier. Richard Randolph of Henrico was granted ten thousand acres much of it located in what is now Franklin County; he in turn sold grants of land to those brave enough to come to the wilderness and to try to tame it.

After 1741, the southwestern area of the county saw these courageous first settlers claiming plots of lands ranging from a few acres to hundreds of acres. It should be noted that while there were no local Native Americans left to harass these early settlers, still other bands from the Ohio Valley periodically launched raids, especially during the French and Indian War (1756-1763). Robert Hill who settled on the Pigg River near present day Rocky Mount is said to have lost two sons to warring Shawnees around 1757. In 1758, Shawnees abducted the Robert Pusey family from their home on Otter Creek some eight miles west of present day Ferrum and held them until 1764 (Salmon 31).

Among the stalwart early settlers in what would become the Ferrum community were Jacob Atkins, William Mavity, Robert Mavity, William Ferguson, John Jones, Thomas Jones, Samuel Darst, William Cook, Roger Turner, Owen Ruble, Easom Slone, Mordecai Mosley and Edgecomb

Figure 2.   A section of the Franklin County Historical Society Settlement Map showing the family names of some of the earliest settlers (1786 - 1886) in western Franklin County.

4

Guilliams (As shown on The Franklin County Settlement Map (1786-1886) prepared by the Franklin County Historical Society in 1976). Some of these settlers came westward from the English Colony in Tidewater Virginia along the Warwick Road which was the antecedent of U.S. Route 460. A road leading southward into what would become Franklin County in 1786 branched off the Warwick Road near New London and followed a course that included parts of modern Virginia Route 122. The road variously known as the Great Warriors Trace, the Great Wagon Road, and the Carolina Road brought German and Scots-Irish settlers from Pennsylvania down the Shenandoah Valley and Roanoke Valley into Franklin County through Maggoty Gap near Boones Mill and continued southward on to the Carolinas.

Most of the people who chose to settle in southwestern Franklin County were the descendants of the hardy Scots-Irish who were looking for land away from direct English control. That much of the land consisted of rocky, steep hillsides did not deter these folks. In the end they struck an uneasy and impermanent bargain with the Colonial government that essentially stated if you leave us alone, we in turn will guard the frontier (J. Webb 144-45).

The land on which the village of Ferrum is situated was granted to William Mavity (McVeaty) and William Ferguson in 1782 in a grant of 1456 acres. Jacob Atkins was granted 404 acres in 1779; Ferrum College most probably occupies this land today. To the west of the Atkins' land, the Drurys, Haynes, and William Pinckard families had holdings dating from 1777. To the east of the Atkins' land were 362 acres granted to Phillip Sheridan in 1779. To the northeast along present Rte. 864 (Old Ferrum Road) and Story Creek, Hugh Neal owned forty-five acres (1795). The potter Samuel Durst originally owned thirteen acres, but before his death in 1791 he had acquired an additional 220 acres which included the site of the Carron Iron Works on Story Creek (Salmon 33). William Cook, for whom presumably Cook's Knob is named, acquired a patent for 187 acres on the north side of the Knob in 1769. To the southeast of present-day Ferrum, Robert Blakley bought 253 acres in 1779 and John Fuson 329 acres in 1772. To the south Mordecai Mosely was granted land in 1780. To the west of the present village Thomas Jones acquired 507 acres in 1789. (Note: Much of the preceding information on eighteenth century land grants and patents was based on research done by a team led by Anne Carter Lee Gravely in the 1970's.)

All of these settlers would have built simple log dwellings with wood shingle roofs and packed clay floors. Either a stick and mud or a stone fireplace and chimney would have served for cooking and heating. A hand dug well or, more likely, a spring would have supplied water. Inventories from the period reveal minimal furnishings consisting of stools, tables, benches, rope beds, corn shuck pallets, simple hand tools, cooking utensils, wooden buckets, wooden bowls and spoons. Guns were expensive and often did not appear on inventories because they were passed down from father to son. Barns were built later when farmers could afford to build them. Before barns and fences livestock including cows, horses, pigs and sheep were marked with ear slits and allowed to roam (Salmon 33).

As the nineteenth century dawned most of these settlers continued to eke out barely more than a subsistence level living, but they persevered, raised their families, welcomed newcomers, sold, traded, or expanded their lands. Little changed for these people until the Civil War and Reconstruction when arguably times got more difficult as money and even food became scarcer. For western Franklin County significant material improvement in the standard of living did not occur until the 1890's with the coming of the railroad and the founding of a small but vibrant commercial village.

Chapter 2

It Takes a Railroad to Raise a Village

The village of Ferrum (36 55' 35" N, 80 0' 40" W) lies in the foothills of the Blue Ridge Mountains and is situated in an area of low hills and narrow valleys with small streams trickling through them. (see ch. 9, fig. 2) The largest stream is Story (Starry) Creek, a tributary of the Pigg River some two miles distance to the northeast. With its headwaters just to the west of the village, the creek skirts the north end of the village before turning northeast to merge with the Pigg River near Rocky Mount. Five miles to the northeast, the historic Carolina Road crosses the Pigg at the site of the Waid Stagecoach Stop and makes it way southward coming to within three miles of Ferrum. The more prominent isolated, rounded hills or knobs were named for early residents (Saul's Knob, Haynes' Knob, Cook's Knob and Jamison's Knob). To the consternation of some, Saul's Knob was rechristened Ferrum Mountain in the twentieth century. To the south the long low ridge of Brown Hill runs southwest toward the Smith River (shown as the Irvine (Irwin) River on the earliest maps of the area). The village sits in a valley with an elevation of 1,235 feet. A scant fifteen miles to the west is the crest of the Blue Ridge with an average elevation between 3,000 and 4,000 feet.

Ferrum had its beginning with the building of the Roanoke and Southern Railroad (1888-1892). Before the railroad and its passenger and freight station, the small valley was home to a few scattered farms

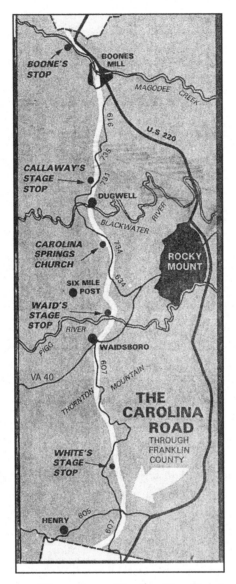

*Figure 1.   The Carolina Road
runs through Franklin County; Roanoke
Times September 2, 1984.*

*Figure 2.   The Ferrum railroad station as it appeared in 1890's.
(Courtesy of the Blue Ridge Institute)*

with the Elkanah Keys farm (originally the Mavity and some of the Ferguson properties) being the largest and closest to the railroad right of way. The station and village could have been named Keys as it was common practice to name the station after the nearest principal land owner, e.g., Starkey, Wirtz, Bassett. The name Ferrum (Latin for iron) was chosen when iron ore was discovered in the Flint Hill (Summit) Cut just south of the station by the railroad surveyors (P. Slone, Monograph 4). One story, probably apocryphal, credits the naming of the station to the original railroad surveyors who repeatedly shouted, "Ferrum, ferrum!" in disgust when their instruments kept being affected by the iron deposits along the right of way. Another explanation is offered by Dr. Frank B. Hurt in a 1974 monograph, "History of (the) Village of Ferrum." Hurt writes that the Methodist minister Thomas Duke, a graduate of Randolph Macon Men's College and a man versed in Latin, proposed the name of Ferrum precisely because of the proliferation of iron in the area (Hurt,"Reflections" 10). In any case, by 1892 both the railroad station and the post office were designated as Ferrum as was the village that grew around them. In addition to Elkanah Keys, the other land owners in the area, some descendants of the original eighteenth and early nineteenth century German and Scots-Irish settlers, included Peter Young (heirs:

11

Jehu Young, Robert Young (1846-1921), and Lewis Young; Sarah Angle (1843-1917)); A.D. Beckner; Samuel Ward(1823-1892) (heirs: Mrs. William Feazelle nee Sarah Elizabeth Ward (1846-1927) and Mrs. Thomas Page Duke nee Jennie Ward); Cyrus Pinckard; and John Jamison (Slone 3). Dr. Frank Hurt in his *A History of Ferrum College* lists the following families as making up the population of about 300 people of

Figure 3.   The tombstone of Elkanah Keys (1838-1913) is located on Nolen's Hill Road overlooking the village. (Courtesy of the Blue Ridge Institute)

Figure 4.   The William Matt Feazelle log house (photo circa 1910) stood on the present day Ferrum College campus near Franklin Hall. (Courtesy of the Blue Ridge Institute)

the village in 1913: Sauls, Beckners, Wards, Drewerys, Hickmans, Jamisons, Youngs, Angles, Wades, Pinckards, Martins, Keyes, Turners, Buckners, Feazelles, Fergusons, Menefees, Nolens, Hurts, Goodes, Shivelys, Lemons, Slones, Brammers, Nicholsons, Ingrams, Stanleys, Scotts, Browns, and Woods (23).

Black families have always played an important part in the history of Ferrum. That the surnames of many of these families bear similarity to the aforementioned white settlers and landowners is no coincidence, rather it is the consequence of slavery. With Emancipation at the end of the Civil War in 1865, Black families often took the surnames of their former masters. More often than not, especially if their masters had been reasonably kind, these newly freed slaves, having few if any other options, simply continued to work for their former owners. Eventually, many were able to buy land, sometimes the very land they or their parents had labored on as slaves. So it is not unexpected that many of the names of Black families echo the names of Keys, Ferguson, Turner, Young, Menefee, Lemon, Brown and Wade. None of these families, however, lived in the village proper as segregation was the law of the land and social norms prevented the races from living in close proximity to one another. The Ben Turner family lived about one half mile southwest of Ferrum on Flint Hill near Timberline Road. Albert Brown, his wife Elizabeth Turner Brown (affectionately known as "Miss" or "Aunt" Lizzie), and family lived in a large four square brick house a half mile to the east of the village on Rte. 40. She worked as cook and domestic worker for local white families well into the 1950's. He farmed several acres adjacent to his house and for a short while operated a small store near his home. Their descendants still own and live on the property. Most of the Black families, including the Youngs, the Keys, and the Fergusons, lived to the west of the village along what is today King Richard Road.

Figure 5.   The Albert and Elizabeth Brown farm property located across from the Ferrum Rescue Squad building is still owned by the Brown descendants. (Courtesy of the Blue Ridge Institute)

Chapter 3

The Merchants: First Among Equals

Among the early landowners were ambitious and entrepreneurial men who saw the commercial opportunities that the railroad would bring to this remote and previously isolated corner of Franklin County. Tracing the history of the various retail businesses they founded in Ferrum, however, is complicated by takeovers, bankruptcies, mergers, buyouts, acquisitions, partnerships, and family connections. Untangling them in the absence of complete records is difficult. The county only required a legal record for businesses organized by more than one person. The *Partnership Books* (#1, #2, and A) in the office of the Clerk of the Circuit Court record the formation of partnerships and corporations from 1890 to the 1950's. The businesses had to be designated by a name, the officers and Board of Directors had to be listed, and the nature of the enterprise had to be described in some detail. Those businesses owned by an individual were not required to register or secure a license.

Operating a business even in a small village was not without its challenges. Chief among these was fierce competition even in the early days. Merchants tried to cultivate relationships with the farmers and lumbermen who brought in produce, chestnuts, livestock, tanbark, railroad crossties, mine props, lumber, telegraph poles, and other products to sell or barter. If the seller did not have a preferred merchant, one he trusted or one to whom he perhaps owed money, the merchant buyers

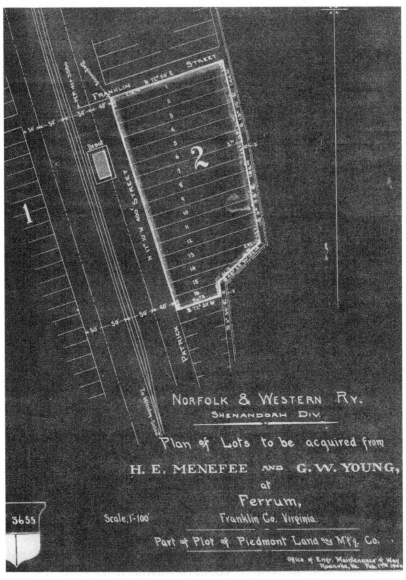

Figure 1.   A 1902 Piedmont Land and Manufacturing Company plat for the area around the Ferrum railroad station. (Franklin County, Va Circuit Court Clerk's Office)

had to bid on the products. The merchant wanted to accumulate enough crossties, props, poles, tan bark, etc., to fill a railroad car for shipment to buyers and realize a tidy profit in the bargain.

The Ferrum merchants were among the most prosperous members of the community as evidenced by the comfortable homes they built for themselves and their families and, in some cases, by their other financial interests such as the telephone company, the bank, and later the veneer plant or the silk mill.

Figure 2.   Photo of an early Ferrum lumber company. (Courtesy of Kitty Martin.)

As early as 1893, Giles W.B. Hale, a founder and early mayor of Rocky Mount, operated the Franklin Log and Lumber Company at Ferrum buying and selling timber (Salmon 340). Seizing on the opportunity to sell land in lots close to the new railroad station, H.E. Menefee and G.W. Young formed the Piedmont Land and Manufacturing Company. A plat dated February 19, 1902, from the Franklin County Circuit Court Clerk's files shows a grid laid out with 16 lots to the east of the station and a street designated as Patrick running north to south paralleling the railroad tracks and a street designated as Franklin running east to west perpendicular to the tracks.

Among the earliest store owners was George Menefee, who built a frame store building on the east side of the railroad tracks a hundred yards south of the Roanoke and Southern station. Menefee was in business by 1890, but by 1893 he was bankrupt and had to sell his property to repay his numerous creditors. Among the creditors were Roanoke Grocery and Milling Company; Weisiger Clothing Company of Richmond; Guggenhiemer and Company of Lynchburg; Harris Snyder Basset and

Company of Philadelphia, PA; J.F. Stratton Company, New York and eleven other companies and individuals for a total at the time of $2344. In today's dollars the debt would be equal to approximately $60,000. The Deed of Trust in the *Franklin County Deed Book* (44:215) describes the stock of the general merchandise business as consisting of dry goods, notions, boots, shoes, hats, groceries and other goods. This list and the diversity of the suppliers/creditors speak to the variety of goods on offer in Ferrum even at this early date.

Just as today, small businesses then faced a high probability of failure for a host of reasons, not the least of which was the failure of customers to pay their bills. Because of the real scarcity of cash, merchants were forced to barter or sell on credit and hope to collect later. If the debtor paid his bills in a timely manner, the merchant could pay his suppliers and all was well; if not, the merchant would be forced into insolvency as was George Menefee. This precarious way of doing business probably explains why merchants who bought goods from customers to insist on barter or payment in store script or due bills that were only good for purchases in that merchant's store.

Another victim of bankruptcy was George Turner who built his store in 1888 on the headwaters of Story Creek about a mile west of present day Ferrum.

Turner lost both his store business and his newly granted post office franchise due to an unfortunate combination of factors. The first cause was customers who would not or could not pay their bills. The second and decisive cause was the irreversible loss of his entire stock of goods in 1891 when thieves stripped his shelves bare and hauled everything away in wagons (Drewery 73-74).

Ironically, it was the equally ill-fated George Menefee store that was the successor to Turner's post office. George Menefee's wife Florence N. Menefee has the distinction of being the first post master (mistress) of Ferrum, Virginia. George Menefee like many ambitious and motivated

Figure 3. *The George Menefee house as it appeared in 2019.*
(Courtesy of the Blue Ridge Institute)

men when knocked down by adversity simply got up again. In 1896 he is listed as one of the founders of the Ferrum Stave Manufacturing Company. His handsome white frame house still stands high on a hill overlooking the village near the Menefee family cemetery. The extended Menefee family can trace its ancestors to the original seventeenth century Virginia settlers. The Menefee family at one time laid claim to a large part of the area that modern Richmond occupies. In Franklin County the family owned a large plantation south of Rocky Mount.

Following the closing of the George Menefee store, Walter H. Nolen bought the business and built a two-story addition (P. Slone, Monograph 11). No record could be found of the first name of Nolen's business. In 1917 sometime after Nolen's death, his widow's second husband, J.O. Boothe along with D.A. Nicholson, W.T. Ingram and some other prominent Franklin County businessmen including Jack Garst of Boones Mill and S.S. Guerrant of Callaway organized the Ferrum Supply Corporation. *Partnership Book #1* describes the purpose of the business as "to buy and sell at retail and wholesale groceries, feed, fertilizer, machinery, farmer's supplies, clothing, shoes, and other merchandise."

To handle such an array of goods the original building was again

21

Figure 4.   Ferrum Supply Company in the 1920's clearly showing the additions to the original George Menefee store. (Courtesy of the Blue Ridge Institute)

enlarged and a much larger building was constructed just to the north of this building. Later a warehouse was built on the south side of the original building. A small frame post office building was constructed next door to the Ferrrum Supply Store on the south side by the main road (Rte.40); the warehouse with its barred windows stood just behind the post office.

All of the village businesses would serve a growing clientele who traveled to Ferrum from western Franklin County as well as eastern Floyd County and south western Patrick County. The patrons of these businesses had for the time an amazing choice of goods, and Gladys Edwards Willis shows how sophisticated the array of merchandise had become by the 1920's when she writes, "Ferrum even had a millinery shop...a milliner at the Ferrum Mercantile made lovely chapeaux for the more affluent ladies in the area."(42). *The Virginia Business Directory of 1917* reports that the only florist in the county was B.M. Buckhorn of Ferrum (Salmon 351).

Business stationery and copies of statements from various Ferrum

Figure 5. *The Ferrum railroad crossing shown in the winter of 1929. (Courtesy of the Blue Ridge Institute)*

businesses exist from as early as 1908. One such statement from 11/30/1908 shows that H.E. Menefee and Company: General Merchandise specialized in dealing in tanbark and cross-ties and were agents for J.I. Nissen Round and Square Hound Wagons. Apparently, the 1917 Ferrum Supply Corporation cited above was not the first incarnation of a business with the Ferrum Supply name. A 1912 statement exists from Ferrum Supply Co.: General Merchandise--Shippers of Apples in Car Lots with a hand stamped motto "Your Credit Is Good, But We Need Money." A surviving price and specification list for telegraph poles of various lengths provides a rather expansive description of the commercial interests of The Ferrum Supply Company in June of 1914. According to the information in the letterhead of this list, the company dealt in wholesale produce, general merchandise to include clothing, hats, ladies' dress goods, and Star Brand shoes. In addition they bought and sold apples, hay, grain, flour, fertilizer, tan bark, poplar and chestnut wood as well as J.I. Nissen wagons. The owners of this Ferrum Supply Company are listed as D.A. Nicholson, T.C. Nicholson, and J.H. Nicholson in the letterhead. To add to the confusion this price list had an envelope attached to it with the return address of Nicholson & Menefee Lumber with Ferrum Supply Company hand stamped over it. Yet another

FERRUM SUPPLY COMPANY
GENERAL MERCHANTS
FURNITURE A SPECIALTY

H. E. MENEFEE & CO.
GENERAL MERCHANDISE
AGENTS J. I NISSER ROUND AND SQUARE HOUND
WAGONS

TAN BARK AND CROSS-TIES
A SPECIALTY

FERRUM, VA., ... 190_

FERRUM, VA. *Feby 10th* 1916

M_ *A. J. Hurt*

Ferrum, Va.

GEO. E. NISSEN WAGONS
HAMPTON BUGGIES
AGRICULTURAL MACHINERY
ENGINES, BOILERS
CEMENT, LIME
FERTILIZER, ETC, ETC.

BOUGHT OF
HURT & COMPANY
WHOLESALE AND RETAIL
DEPARTMENT STORE
BUYERS OF COUNTRY PRODUCE, CROSS-TIES, TAN-BARK, ETC.

MANUFACTURERS OF
LOCUST AND OAK INSULTING
PINS, AND OAK BRACKETS
HIGH-GRADE MEAL
AND CHOP
STANDARD CANNED GOODS

D. A. NICHOLSON, PRESIDENT   W. T. INGRAM, VICE-PRESIDENT   Y. C. NICHOLSON, SEC'Y-TREAS

DIRECTORS
DR. S. S. GUERRANT H. E. MENEFEE
DR. T. F. ARTHUR   W. T. INGRAM
JACK DARST   D. A. NICHOLSON
T. C. NICHOLSON   C. A. HICKMAN
HARDIN INGRAM   R. A. BARNHART

FERRUM SUPPLY CORPORATION
WHOLESALE & RETAIL MERCHANTS
MANUFACTURERS SLACK BARREL STAVES AND HEADINGS
APPLE AND FLOUR BARRELS
CANNERS OF TOMATOES, ETC.
FERRUM, VA.

WHOLESALE
APPLES
PRODUCE
FLOUR AND
APPLE BARRELS
CANNED GOODS

D. A. NICHOLSON   T. C. NICHOLSON   J. H. NICHOLSON

SPECIALTIES:
Apples
Hay, Grain
and Flour

FERRUM SUPPLY COMPANY
Wholesale Produce Dealers ❖ General Merchandise
CLOTHING, HATS, LADIES' DRESS GOODS.   STAR BRAND SHOES FOR ALL THE FAMILY

Fertilizers and
J I. Nissen Wagons
Tan Bark, Poplar
and Chestnut Wood

*Figure 6.   Assorted letterheads from early Ferrum businesses.
(Courtesy of the Franklin County Historical Society)*

24

Figure 7.   *David A. Nicholson House as it appeared in 2019.*
(Courtesy of the Blue Ridge Institute)

Ferrum Supply Company statement from January 7, 1915, still lists the Nicholsons as owners but pares down the business description to wholesale produce dealers and general merchants with a specialty in apples and canned goods in car lots. Whether financial reversals occurred is unknown, but reorganization definitely occurred in 1917.

In the 1917 incorporation the Nicholson family still retained a financial interest in the business sufficiently strong for D.A. Nicholson to be named president of the "new" business. A 1921 Ferrum Supply Corporation—Wholesale and Retail Merchants statement reflects a somewhat revitalized business. In addition to buying and selling apples, produce, flour, canned goods and apple barrels, they had expanded into manufacturing slack barrel staves, and headings and operating a cannery for tomatoes and other vegetables and fruits. In hindsight it is probably not hard to see that the 1920's may not have been the most auspicious time to make a major investment in barrel making. Though to be fair, Dr. S.S. Guerrant, who not coincidentally was a director of the corporation, was shipping twenty-thousand barrels of apples in 1933 from his

Figure 8.   Ferrum Garage and Ferrum Mercantile Company as it appeared in 1960's. (Courtesy of David Clements)

Callaway orchards (Salmon 372).

On April 26, 1928, the Ferrum Supply Corporation changed its name to Ferrum Mercantile Company, Inc. with new owners: Guy W. Nolen and C.B. Nolen, both sons of Walter H. Nolen, A.H. Shively and G.L. Martin. The purpose of the business given in the *Partnership Book* was "to purchase, sell and deliver any such goods, groceries, hardware supplies, and merchandise as are and to buy, sell, rent, store, and repair and care for motor vehicles of all kinds and supplies." From this description it is clear that the Mercantile included Ferrum Garage and the Chevrolet dealership that would operate in Ferrum until the 1960's. To obtain a Chevrolet dealership the franchisees had to meet certain criteria such as operate a garage that employed a General Motors certified mechanic who periodically attended additional training sessions. Other requirements specified the minimum square footage for an indoor showroom and the square footage of plate glass display windows visible from the street. The Ferrum dealership installed the requisite plate glass windows on the second floor of one of the original Ferrum Supply structures which was thereafter known as the Chevrolet Building. Thus the requirement was met, but probably not in the way General Motors had intended.

Ferrum Mercantile was ensnared in the federal liquor conspiracy trial of 1935. The Corporation itself and the principals were indicted and tried as participants in the conspiracy "to defraud the United States of America" of lawful taxes (Greer, *Conspiracy* 47-48). All eventually changed their pleas from not guilty to nolo contendere and received the following fines: Ferrum Mercantile Company, Inc.-$3,000; Grover L. Martin-$500; C. Buford Nolen- $500; Guy W. Nolen- $500: Herman Shively-$2,500 (Greer *Conspiracy* 615). The $3,000 fine imposed in 1935 would be the equivalent of about $50,000 today.

In November of 1941 the same group of owners reorganized again and named the business Ferrum Mercantile Company and Ferrum Garage (*Partnership Book #1* 35). In March of 1955, a sworn affidavit in *Partnership Book #2* declares that G.L. Martin has withdrawn from the partnership and that C.B. Nolen has become an inactive partner leaving G.W. Nolen and A.H. Shively as the active partners (11). When Shively relocated to Alta Vista in 1959, G.W. Nolen became the owner of the business. While Ferrum Garage operated for a few more years, Nolen liquidated Ferrum Mercantile in the early 1960's ending the seventy-year saga of the mercantile business begun by Nolen's father, W.H. Nolen. In a curious twist of history, Nolen leased the Mercantile building to Jack Menefee who opened a short-lived grocery store; Menefee was the son of George Menefee, the man who had been forced to sell that first Ferrum store to Nolen's father in 1893.

Prior to his death at the relatively young age of forty-six in 1905, Walter Nolen built a handsome two-story frame house in sight of his store building, a few hundred yards east of the railroad crossing. Ever the entrepreneurs, Nolen and his wife took advantage of their proximity to the new railroad station and used their large residence as a rooming and boarding house. Some years after Mr. Nolen's death, his widow Berta Saul Nolen married John Boothe and lived there well into her eighties dying in 1960.

By 1905 John Kemper Hurt had built a large two-story frame general

Figure 9.   The house of Walter H. and Berta Saul Nolen (circa 1900) was located just to the east of the railroad station. (Courtesy of Belle Nolen Cooper)

merchandise store directly across from the railroad crossing on the west side. Hurt proved to be an extraordinary entrepreneur founding many different enterprises under the umbrella of Hurt and Company. In addition to the original dry goods and general merchandise business, he operated a retail and wholesale grocery store, a feed and grain store, a hardware store, a jewelry store, a drug store, a café/tearoom, and a garage; he also sold building supplies, lime and fertilizer, farm supplies, and agricultural machinery, Nissen Wagons and Hampton Buggies, engines and boilers, as well as oil, kerosene and gasoline. He owned the Ferrum Furniture Company in partnership with Dr. Benjamin M. Beckham and W. Bunyan Thompson. He bought and shipped tanbark, cross ties, lumber, telegraph and telephone poles, and farm produce and livestock. He manufactured locust and oak insulating pins and oak brackets that were used on telegraph and telephone poles. He operated a grist mill. He established a cannery and shipped canned tomatoes and fruit by the railcar load. He was a director of the Peoples National Bank in 1907 in Rocky Mount. He helped to found the Bank of Ferrum in 1916. He

Figure 10.   J.K. Hurt Store circa 1913. (Courtesy of the Blue Ridge Institute)

Figure 11.   J.K. Hurt and Company shown here after the 1930 remodeling. (Courtesy of the Blue Ridge Institute)

Figure 12. *The interior of J.K. Hurt's Ferrum Drug Company as it appeared in the 1930's. (Courtesy of the Blue Ridge Institute)*

provided the land on which the original bank building was constructed in 1917. That this land was surrounded by several Hurt and Company buildings and businesses was probably no coincidence.

In 1930 Hurt added a fine two-story brick façade to the original store building which sat on the main trackside street opposite the railroad crossing. The improvements included multiple large plate glass windows and arched doorways. Given the Stock Market Crash of 1929 and the Depression that followed, perhaps 1930 was not the most opportune time to undertake such a largely cosmetic remodeling project. Pictures of the finished building show a one-hundred-foot building as handsome and well-designed as any in Franklin County rivaling even the Angle Block in Rocky Mount which, of course, belonged to Hurt's brother-in-law, Nathaniel Angle. Whether his decision to remodel was wise or not, prudent or imprudent, he did not live to see his businesses in particular

Figure 13.   *The J.K. Hurt house located just west of the village. (Courtesy of the Blue Ridge Institute)*

and the country as a whole struggle through the Great Depression of the 1930's. Sadly, he died by his own hand in 1932. Nor did he have to witness his life's work burn in March of 1940. Hurt and Company died in the flames of that windy night and could not phoenix-like rise from the ashes.

It should not go unremarked upon that neither J.K. Hurt nor Hurt and Company rated so much as a mention in Keister Greer's *The Great Moonshine Conspiracy Trial of 1935*. That Hurt and Company could remain untainted by the conspiracy that was swirling about it admittedly beggars belief, but the record does not reflect any involvement. The only mention of Hurt and Company in the *Roanoke Times* coverage of the 1935 trial comes in a general listing of virtually all Franklin County stores. No inference of involvement in the conspiracy was drawn by either the newspaper or the court (Stephenson 65-67). The fact remains that no one associated with Hurt and Company was charged, indicted, or convicted of anything. As noted, other Ferrum merchants and businesses were ensnared by the federal investigation, convicted of conspiracy, and drew large fines and/or prison sentences.

Another prominent Ferrum businessman W. Bunyan Thompson did

Figure 14. The Thompson building (circa 1927) as it appeared in 2019. (Courtesy of the Blue Ridge Institute)

not survive the financial reverses of the late 1920's. Thompson was a founding director of the Ferrum bank and builder of one of the finest buildings in the village, one that was architecturally superior even to the Hurt Block. The Thompson building survives though diminished somewhat by clumsy remodeling that did not preserve its original tall second floor diamond paned swing out windows. The addition of an unattractive single floor structure to the south side of the building further compromised the appearance of the original edifice. The first floor of the building housed two stores each with two large plate glass windows facing the street. On the second floor were at least three residential apartments. After the 1940 fire, Mary Hurt Whitehead operated a drug store on these premises, and Dr. J.M. Green used the addition as a medical office. For many years Claire and Elma Scott Young ran a hardware store and a grocery store here. In more recent times a succession of restaurants, including Mama Kay's, Shiners, and the Paradise Sports Grill, have operated on this site.

Marshall Wingfield in his *History of Franklin County* described the village in 1935 as consisting of "three general merchandise stores, two wholesale grocery stores, two drug stores, one restaurant, two barber shops, one undertaking establishment, one lumber and pin mill, two grist mills, two garages, an automobile sales agency, one furniture and hardware store, two physicians' offices, and wholesale gasoline distributing tanks…" (64).

Interestingly, he omits any reference to the Bank of Ferrum which was organized and built on the lot donated by J.K. Hurt in 1917. He also omits the Pool Room, the very existence of which may have offended his Presbyterian minister's sensibilities.

In his 1955 monograph on Ferrum Pedro Slone states that soon after the acquisition of the George Menefee store by W. H. Nolen in the early 1890's, another store building was erected on the west side of the railroad tracks by Henry M. Turner and Berkley Price (11-12). Slone lists the following men who operated general merchandise stores in Ferrum : George. A. Menefee, Walter H. Nolen, Henry Turner and Berkley Price, D.A. Nicholson (1875-1945) and Albert Lafayette Lemons(1869-1931), Goode Brothers, Henry Eldridge Menefee (1868-1922), W.C. Cousens, M.D., John Kemper Hurt (1873-1932), William H. Buckner (1858-1944), Charles A. Hickman (1869-1941), Judson Mullins, Guy Nolen (Ferrum Mercantile), Ernest Buford Easter (1904-1975) (Nicholson Grocery Company), Clarie Young (1904-1975) (Young's Hardware and Grocery),T. Marvin Mason (1903-1984), and Rufus L. Ferguson (1880-1956). In addition he lists Mary Whitehead as proprietor of Ferrum Drug Company and V.E. Austin (1907-1980) as owner of a plumbing supply business. Slone states that "There has only been one drug store…" contradicting the Wingfield account of two drug stores (P. Slone, Monograph 12). Wingfield was correct, however, as J.A. Moore did operate the Peoples Pharmacy in the 1930's down the street south of J.K. Hurt's Ferrum Drug Company.

The Turner and Price store was located on the south end of the trackside businesses on the west side of the railway crossing. A Norfolk and Western Engineering and Maintenance of Way drawing from 1898 shows a Thornton's Store (almost certainly owned by William L. Thornton) on this site that would have preceded the Price and Turner business. This location saw a succession of stores and related owners.

Figure 15.   The house of H.E. and Lew Angle Menefee as it appeared in 2019. (Courtesy of the Blue Ridge Institute)

Following Turner and Price, C.A. Hickman (husband of Berta Turner), operated this general merchandise store. Henry E. Menefee owned the trackside property on the west side of the railroad tracks to the south of the Turner Price store. In addition to his own fine two-story frame house, Menefee owned several other buildings between the residence and the Turner Price store. Although this store was operated continuously for almost fifty years by the allied William Thornton, Henry Turner, Charles A. Hickman and Judson Mullins families with the Menefees until the fire of 1940, the H. E. Menefee family had sole control of the land after the fire. The C.A. Hickman store stood at the extreme southern end of the track side business block; photographs reveal the store to be a white wood frame two-story structure with additional smaller buildings to the side and rear. This store and all its out buildings were destroyed in the 1940 fire.

After the 1940 fire, Mrs. Henry E. Menefee built a large single story brick structure with four store fronts anchoring this corner of the village. A series of grocery stores were operated on this site beginning with Judson Mullins (1887-1961), Ernest B. Easter (1904-1975) and Dillard Nicholson, and Frank Peters. Other businesses located in this building

Figure 16.   The second brick Menefee building was built in the early 1940's. (Courtesy of David Clements)

Figure 17.   The remodeled Menefee building currently houses apartments. (Courtesy of the Blue Ridge Institute)

Figure 18.   The William H. Buckner house still stands about one mile southwest of the village. (Courtesy of the Blue Ridge Institute)

included a restaurant operated among others by J.M. Manor, Myrtle Menefee Bowles, Clydie Mullins, Dewey Nolen, Oscar Flemon (Mutt) Cannaday (1893-1978), Leslie Carter, and Alfred and Ruby Martin Skinnell and Wilbur Woods; a pool room operated by Henry "Boo" Menefee; a U.S. Post Office; V.A. Dodson and Ted Boyd's barbershop; Glen Carter's watch repair shop. Today, the building houses several residential apartments. William H. Buckner ran his general merchandise store and a livery business on Rte.623 near his home which still stands about one mile from the south end of the village.

Prior to 1940 the center section of the trackside businesses was dominated by Hurt and Company, the previously described diversified enterprise selling everything from groceries to hardware to jewelry to drugs to bulk livestock feed. To the south, adjacent to Hurt and Company was the Ferrum Pool Room operated by among others Walter Edwards and later Jack Menefee in 1940. To the north of Hurt and Company was the original Ferrum Bank (1917). To the north of the bank was the Hurt Garage a large, single-story tin covered structure with an attached wood frame gasoline filling station with a large canopied roof extending out to

Figure 19.   Claire Young's Service Station c. 1960 (Courtesy of the Blue Ridge Institute)

the street so gas could be pumped in all weather. Behind this garage complex stood the gasoline and kerosene storage tanks of the Hurt Wholesale Fuel business. At some point in the 1930's, Guy Nolen acquired the fuel business and employed Fred Ingram as the delivery truck driver. According to Colonel James Stanley, the Standard Oil Company eventually forced Nolen to relinquish his franchise, but paid him the princely sum of $50 per month for ten years much to the astonishment, and perhaps envy, of the locals.

About 1928 Claire Young bought the Hurt Garage and Filling Station. The old garage building was used as a Ford dealership in the 1950's by D.M. "Doc" Ramsey, W.E. Stanley and William Bullock. Young added a cinder block garage complex to the north of the filling station. The old bank building and the tin garage building were razed in the late 1960's; in 1970 Hugh and Shirley Young Green built a large single story brick building and operated Green's Pharmacy there until 2003. Since that time, the building has housed a restaurant, a collectibles business, a thrift shop, and a cake shop (H. Green).

To the north of the Hurt/Young garage complex and adjacent to the Thompson Building, Marvin Brammer operated a garage from the early

Figure 20.   The Green's Pharmacy building was erected in 1970 on the site of the 1917 bank building. (Courtesy of Blue Ridge Institute)

1950's until 1976. A fruit and vegetable cannery stood near this site in 1914 as did a small packing house (warehouse) owned by Paul Simms. This packing house was later moved a few yards north on to land owned by Pedro Slone and was used by the Ferrum Boy Scout Troup 32 as a meeting house for years.

At the north end of the trackside business block on the west side of the railroad stood D.A. Nicholson's Wholesale Grocery Store, a large wood frame building with a tin roof. T. Marvin Mason ran a grocery store here in the 1940's and 1950's. Before the building was razed to make way for the "77" Restaurant building and parking lot, Eugene Quinn operated a used clothing and furniture store there. Paul and Hettie Radford built the "77" Restaurant and opened for business on January 1, 1960. They named the restaurant after his Number "77" race car. In 1966 Wallace and Dot Dalton bought the restaurant and adjoining Barber Shop operated by Layman Sigmon. In the 1950's, Sim Wade built and ran a small grocery store at the extreme northern end of the village at the intersection of the Old Ferrum Road (Rte.864) and Rte. 40 (now Timberline Road). The Sheriff Shively Bridge carries Rte. 40 over the site now.

Slone notes the Bank of Ferrum was organized in 1917 and became the National Bank in 1920 with the following presidents: B.M. Beckham, W. Bunyan Thompson (1885-1929), R.A. Barnhart, and John D. Burnett

Figure 21.   The "77" Restaurant was opened by Paul and Heddy Radford on January 1, 1960. Since 1966 the restaurant has been operated by the Wallace Dalton family. (Courtesy of Lloyd Edwards)

(1892-1970) (P. Slone, Monograph 13). The bank was forced to close March 4, 1933, as part of the federal bank holiday declared by the Franklin Roosevelt administration, but was allowed to reopen after issuing new stock to rebuild capital. While some bank stock-holders lost some of their original investment, no depositor lost any money (K. Goode). The original bank was located to the north of the Hurt Building which was on the west side of the railroad tracks just opposite of the crossing; the new bank building built in 1967 is located four hundred yards to the north of its original location.

Directly behind the original bank building and across a small stream was the voting precinct building (on present Nolen's Hill Road). This small wood frame building was erected in 1920 and replaced the Brown Hill School as the designated voting place for residents of the village (P. Slone, Monograph 10). Given the school was some three miles distance to the south near the Prillaman Switch trestle on Rte. 767, it would seem the precinct location would have been changed years before 1920 to make voting more convenient for the greatest concentration of people in the Brown Hill Magisterial District. That small building served as the official voting site until replaced in the 1950's by a cinderblock building

Figure 22. The First National Bank of Ferrum opened in 1917. (Courtesy of the Blue Ridge Institute)

Figure 23.   In 1967 the First National Bank of Ferrum moved into a new building down the street from its original site. (First National Bank Ad - 1986)

Figure 24.   Today, the bank is a branch of BB&T. (Courtesy of the Blue Ridge Institute)

Figure 25.   A legal tinder five dollar note issued by The First National Bank of Ferrum with the signature of C.L. Ross, cashier. (Ebay)

located on the far north end of the village. In the 1960's a brick structure was built across from Saint James Methodist Church on the site of the old elementary school building. The fire station built on this same site now serves as the voting precinct.

In 1939 Robert DeHart constructed a large tin clad building a few hundred yards to the east of the railroad crossing on present day Rte. 40 adjacent to Saint James Methodist Church. Though it seems incongruous given that the church was so near, the original plan was for the large open space of the building to be used as a dance hall (J.Stanley, Interview). The building eventually housed a general merchandise store and did a brisk business selling sugary treats and snacks to the elementary school children who attended classes in the elementary school just across the street. When the school principal barred the children from leaving the school

Figure 26. *The Robert DeHart building as it appeared in 2019.*
(Courtesy of the Blue Ridge Institute)

playground to visit the DeHart store for treats, Mr. DeHart recaptured the lost business by simply walking across the road at recess and taking "orders" for candy and sodas (D. Mullins). The building was purchased from Dewey Nolen by the church in 1948 and has served over the years as a Sunday school annex, a community center, a craft shop, and a food and clothing distribution center. Until a new parsonage was built in 1961, the second floor apartment of the DeHart Building served as the Methodist parsonage.

Chapter 4

Village Churches

Standing on Rte. 40 just east of the village, the Saint James Methodist Church was built in 1896-1897 and is the oldest surviving structure in the village of Ferrum. In the previous year, a young, newly appointed Methodist minister, Charles Elam Blankenship, along with Church Trustees William L. Thornton, A.L. Lemons, J.R. Foster, George C. Goode, and Dr. J.M. Williams raised over $1,100 toward the cost of a new church. James and Sarah Young Angle donated the one acre lot on which the church was built. The bricks for the church were made near the

Figure 1.   Saint James United Methodist Church (1896-1897) and the adjoining cemetery. (Courtesy of the Blue Ridge Institute)

site and laid by Marshall and Brooks Haynes; I.M. Menefee was the principal carpenter for the project (Merritt 178). The new church, named for Rev. Blankenship's home church in Richmond, replaced the old Rock Spring Methodist Episcopal Church some three miles west of the village on the old wagon road leading to Endicott. In keeping with the Methodist practice of rotating ministers, Rev. Blankenship left his fine new church in 1899; however, he maintained a life-long relationship with the village and its first church by serving for fifty years on the Board of Trustees of Ferrum Training School/College. The following individuals succeeded Rev. Blankenship as ministers at Saint James over the years:

Minister	Years Served
W. C. Pace	1899 - 1901
B. F. Smith	1901 - 1902
James A. Thomas	1902 -1906
R. V. Owen	1906 - 1908
E. S. Hook	1908 - 1909
O. L. Haga	1909 - 1913
F. P. Foust	1913 - 1915
J. W. Bouldin	1915 - 1918
J. W. Lillaston	1918 - 1919
S. A. Wright	1919 - 1920
J. M. Batten	1920 - 1923
B. B. Bland	1923 - 1925
I. L. Llewellen	1924 - 1928
C. L. Morgan	1928 - 1929
R. C. Johnson	1929 - 1931
Charles Boyd	1931 - 1933
J. M. Trower	1933 - 1935
W. B. Estes	1935 - 1936
E. L. Hylton	1936 - 1937
I. L. Llewellen	1937 - 1938

Minister	Years Served
E. K. Emurian	1938 - 1941
M. D. Mitchell	1941 - 1942
J. L. Stone	1942 - 1943
R. L. Tressler	1943 - 1944
James Orser	1944 - 1946
L. P. Jackson	1946 - 1952
Charles Price	1952 - 1954
Alfred Campbell	1954 - 1956
Elmer Thompson	1956 - 1957
William Kelly	1957 - 1958
C. P. Minnick	1958 - 1963
George Wesley Jones	1963 - 1968
Dr. A. E. Acey	1968 - 1973
Lloyd Judy	1973 - 1976
Seneca Foote	1976 - 1979
Herbert G. Hobbs	1979 - 1986
Gordon V. (Ben) Nelson	1986 - 1987
J. Wesley Inge	1987 - 1989
James S. Angle	1989 - 1995
Edward J. Taylor	1995 - 1996
M. G. Goodpasture	1996 - 1998
Wesley Nelson	1998 - 2003
Elizabeth Lazenby	2003 - 2008
Mary S. White	2008 - Present

(J.Stanley, "Saint James" 39-41)

Most of the records of Saint James Church have been lost, but a 1917 Church Registry of members includes the following people, some of whom were among the earliest residents of the community and were founding members of the church in 1897:

Sarah Angle	Goldie Hurt	Clive Pinkard
Berta L. (Nolen) Boothe	Berta Hickman	Gillie Pinkard
Roberta Buckner	Charles Hickman	Della Pinkard
Nannie K. Buckner	Nannie B. Hale	Amanda Pinkard
Nancy A. Buckner	Bettie Hale	John S. Pinkard
Lucy M. Buckner	Pearl F. Hale	Georgie Skinnell
James Buckner	Maude Ingram	R.B. Skinnell
George W. Buckner	Mattie R. Ingram	Pedro T. Slone
Nannie Beckham	Lucy Keith	J. O. Shively
Dora Beckham	Sophia Keys	Dovie L. Rakes
Benjamin M.	Nannie Lemons	Agnes J. Turner
Beckham,Jr.	Albert L. Lemons	Mabel Turner
Dord Barrow	M. O. Lemons	Erie Turnbull
Elva Barrow	Fannie Lemons	Annie Via
Janie H. Bouldin	Gladys Lemons	Mary Angle Wade
Lucy E. Bouldin	Myrtle Lemons	Archie Wagoner
Mildred T. Bouldin	Nannie Matthews	John L. Wagoner
Oscar Chapman	Bernice Menefee	Hairston Wright
George B. Clanton	J.J. Meadows	Maude Wright
John M. Dowdy	D.A. Nicholson	Harry H. Young
Fannie Dowdy	Ida Nicholson	Eula Virginia Davis
Robert R. Dowdy	Essie Nicholson	Exie Katherine Witcher
Mary Belle Dudley	Nola Nicholson	Nettie Dell Shelton
Hellen B. Graves	Albert Nicholson	Zella Irene Young
George Goode	Florence Nicholson	Lucy Doris Shelton
John K. Hurt	Gladys Nicholson	Frances W. Blount
Lelia F. Hurt	Edward Nichols	Bertha M. Stone
Frank Hurt.	Mattie Pinkard	Charles Hugh Allman
Mary Hurt	Myrtle Pinkard	James Wesley Keith
	Richard Aubrey Foster.	

The church has been in continuous use since its dedication in 1897, and members of the congregation and the community still bury

Figure 2. Schoolfield Memorial Chapel is shown here under construction in 1924. (Courtesy of the Blue Ridge Institute)

their dead in the adjoining cemetery. In 1986 when the *Cemetery Records of Franklin County* was published by the Franklin County Historical Society, the Saint James cemetery contained seventy-one graves and was said to have room for at least 420 graves. Given that the church was located on the eastern most side of the lot, it would appear the church founders originally planned for a cemetery to be located on the west side of the lot; the first marked grave though dates from 1917. Some or all of the six unmarked graves could well date from earlier than 1917. Among those interred here include Charles A. Hickman, an early merchant; David A. Nicholson, another early merchant and sheriff of Franklin County as well as a member of the House of Delegates; Charles Lewis Ross, a WWI veteran and longtime banker; Pedro Slone, teacher, mail carrier, and village historian: Leo Scott, founder of Leo Scott Cabinets and KC Farms.

Before the opening of Schoolfield Memorial Chapel in 1925, the students of Ferrum Training School would march in line to Saint James for Sunday services. The congregation of Saint James underwrote one third of the considerable cost of the new campus chapel. With a seating capacity of 500 the chapel was a place of worship but was also a site for

Figure 3.   The Saint James Methodist Church Parsonage on Route 40 was built in 1961. (Courtesy of the Blue Ridge Institute)

cultural events such as lectures, recitals, concerts, choral and dramatic performances that could be shared with the community. In addition, the lower level of the building provided space for a recreational hall, a basketball court, a stage for plays, and even facilities for projecting motion pictures (J. Stanley, "Saint James" 24).

In 1948, the Saint James congregation acquired the adjoining DeHart property including a large metal building and has used it continuously for a variety of church and community purposes including a parsonage, Sunday school classes, church office, Methodist Women and Methodist Youth Fellowship meetings, Boy Scout meetings, and Lions Club meetings, quilting and weaving circles, government programs such as Community Action and Head Start, and even a community credit union. Under the auspices of the federal Community Action program, the Ferrum Craft Shop operated in the building during the 1970's. Lois Scott supervised a number of local quilters who used traditional quilting techniques to produce log cabin style quilts and local weavers who used period looms to weave traditional textiles. Currently, it houses the Saint James Community Mission Center which operates a food bank and clothes closet serving on average forty to fifty families each week. Membership of the church has waxed and waned over the years: 1917-91; 1926-218; 1936-152; 1946-104; 1958-196; 1968-196; 1971-214;

1977-129; 1994-69; 1996-94. Through the dedicated efforts of a small but stalwart congregation, Saint James survives and is, in fact, well into its second century of serving the village.

The Church in collaboration with Ferrum College built a modern brick parsonage in 1961; church member Gail Sigmon who served as general contractor and builder donated all of his labor (J. Stanley, "Saint James" 28). Yet another collaborative project with the college was the construction of Vaughan Memorial Chapel. The Saint James congregation pledged $25,000 in 1967 toward furnishing the Church Educational rooms in the lower level of the Vaughan Chapel. While the joint ventures between the village church and the college have not been without their share of misunderstandings, disappointments and frustrations, the two entities have managed to endure and benefit from each other. Today, a portion of the lower level of the chapel is used by the Tri-Area Community Health Clinic which provides the only medical services to the citizens of the county west of Rocky Mount.

At least one mystery remains. No one seems to know why or how the front of the Methodist Saint James Church features a circular stained glass window that contains what is clearly a Star of David. Though the star is turned on its side, this traditional Jewish symbol has graced Ferrum's oldest building for well over a century with little comment and no known controversy. If I had to hazard a guess, the ever frugal Reverend Mr. Blankenship scooped up this handsome piece of stained glass at a bargain price from a Richmond synagogue sale and brought it to his new church in 1897; with a slight adjustment laterally who was to be the wiser in rural Franklin County. Until a better explanation surfaces, this one

Figure 4.   *The rotated Star of David as it appears in the front gable of the Saint James Methodist Church.*

will have to suffice.

In 1959, the members of a small Church of the Brethren congregation decided to move to Ferrum from New Bethel Church on Republican Church Road a few miles to the southwest. On June 7 of that year they broke ground for a new church atop the hill on Woodcott Road, a few hundred yards to the south of Saint James Church. The congregation

Figure 5.   The First Church of the Brethren of Ferrum as it appeared in 2019. (Courtesy of the Blue Ridge Institute)

purchased three and one-half acres from members of the Will Ross family. The original Bethel church, formed by Benjamin E. Kesler and others, dated from 1887 and was a branch of the Antioch Church of the Brethren in Callaway. (Kesler was the brother of George Thomas Kesler, the local circuit riding Methodist minister who was instrumental in helping Dr. Benjamin Beckham to found Ferrum Training School in 1913.)

On January 8, 1960, Rev. I. D. Hoy, Rev. Arnold Naff, Rev. William Swietzer and Rev. Rufus McDaniel with members of the congregation officially dedicated the First Church of the Brethren of Ferrum. Some of the early members of the church included Flossie Foster, Elvie Kesler Wright, Mildred Young, Marvin Young, George and Vergie Kesler, Earl Scott, George and Willie Young, LeRoy Solomon, Dalton and Nellie

Ferguson, Ronnie Ferguson, Tom and Hilda Wade, Johnny Wade, Laird Bowman, Dewey and Evelina Nolen, Basil and Lucy Quinn.

Among the men who have served this church as ministers are Arnold Naff, I.D. Hoy, Julius Jamison, Lester Hodges, Willard Bowman, Leonard Martin, Michael Pugh, Danny Nolen, Bobby Angel and Gerald Manning as well as Frank Layman, Sr., Frank Layman, Jr., and Ben Layman (grandfather, son, and grandson); the current minister is Ray Bayse (Wright).

In 2009 during the pastorate of Garlin Strouth, the Ferrum Faith Assembly of God Church built a large community ministry center on Rte. 40 just west of the village on the site of the I. W. Ferguson home place. The attractive brick building was built as a ministry outreach center for the home church which was organized in 1964 and is located about seven miles from Ferrum on Thompson Ridge Road. The church generously makes the building available to the Ferrum community for special events.

Figure 6.   The Ferrum Faith Assembly of God Community Ministry Center as it appeared in 2019. (Courtesy of the Blue Ridge Institute)

Chapter 5

The Professionals

Pedro Slone lists eight physicians who had served Ferrum: W.C. Cousens [sic], L.H. Hardie, Walter H. Cobbs (1882-1944), H.L. Poff (1887-1921), F.P. Brammer, W.K. Lloyd, G.W. Boothe, and John Monroe Green (1886- 1975) (P. Slone, Monograph 12). While all of these early doctors would have had medical offices in the village, they made their living by making house calls on horseback, or later, in Model T Fords or other sturdy automobiles to remote homes within a ten-mile radius of Ferrum. Doctor J. M. Williams was practicing medicine in Ferrum in 1896 and, as noted, was instrumental in raising the funds to build Saint James Church; and Dr. William Hairston lived near Hunters Hall at about the same time and is said to have crossed Saul's Knob to tend patients. Dr. Willard C. Cousins practiced in Ferrum around the turn of the twentieth century and was a successful inventor as well as a physician. The August 2009 *The Times of Franklin* contains an article describing Cousins' "Twentieth Century Plow" for which he received a U.S. Patent (#629288) on February 28, 1899. The plow featured a conversion innovation that allowed farmers to change the plow to a single shovel cultivator as well as easily adjust the draft height.

Dr. Poff practiced in Ferrum between 1912 and 1921, and apparently he, too, was an enterprising fellow who bought and subdivided the land on Nolen's Hill into lots and built the large porticoed four-square house

Figure 1.   The Dr. H.L. Poff house, built around 1915, still stands on Nolen's Hill overlooking the village. (Courtesy of the Blue Ridge Institute)

that still stands on the hill. Unfortunately, he met an untimely end when he discovered another man in his wife's bedroom. Gunfire ensued, and the good doctor was killed. Though convicted of murder in his first trial, the shooter claiming self defense was found innocent on appeal. The doctor's house was acquired by A. L. Lemons and was the Lemons family home until the 1990's when it was acquired and restored by Roger and Jacqueline Gillispie. Mark Barnard now owns the house.

According to Cabell F. Cobbs in an August 1987 article in "The Mountain Laurel," his father Dr. Walter Herbert Cobbs practiced medicine in Ferrum for a short while between 1908 and 1912. After serving as a doctor in Shanghai, China in 1913, he returned to Franklin County and established an office in Rocky Mount in 1914 and practiced there until his death in 1944. Dr. William Lloyd practiced in the village in the 1920's. Gladys Edwards Willis remembered her parents thinking highly of Dr. Lloyd not only for his medical skills but for his talent in painting portraits, playing the guitar and even producing and

*Figure 2.   Dr. G.W. Boothe built this house in the 1920's to the
east of the village. (Courtesy of the Blue Ridge Institute)*

performing in community revues (Willis 58). Dr. Lloyd met a tragic
death in an airplane crash sometime after moving his practice from
Ferrum. Dr. Boothe practiced in Ferrum in the 1930's, but he too moved
to Rocky Mount. In the 1950's Dr. William Hughes established a short-
lived medical practice in Ferrum before deciding to move to Boones Mill.
After Dr. Green died in 1975, Dr. J. Francis Amos, Dr. Jack H.
Bumgardner, Dr. John Vaughn, and Dr. Kenneth Lucas established a
satellite of their Rocky Mount office in Green's old office and maintained
a practice in Ferrum until the mid-1980's. More recently, Dr. Donald
Wieble had an office in Ferrum before moving to Rocky Mount. Other
physicians have served in the Tri-Area Community Health Clinic.

The longest serving doctor was Dr. John Monroe Green who practiced
medicine in and around the village for over forty years. In a 1974
interview with the *Martinsville Bulletin*, Dr. Green reminisced about
coming to Ferrum in 1930 to practice medicine. "There were no roads in
those days," he recalled. "I walked to house calls, and I have ridden milk
cows, horses, and steers to get to patients." He remembered charging
$2 for a visit, but he trimmed that back to $1 when times got rough.
He accepted hams, chickens, eggs, old clocks, and dressers among other
things in payment when cash was not in the offing. "I always took

*Figure 3.   Dr. John Monroe Green (1886-1975) practiced
medicine in Ferrum for over forty years. (Courtesy of the Blue Ridge
Institute)*

*Figure 4.   After his office in the J.K. Hurt building (see ch. 3, fig.
11) was destroyed in the fire of 1940, Dr. Green moved his practice
to a small office attached to the Thompson building. (Courtesy of the
Blue Ridge Institute)*

Figure 5.   Dr. Green lived in this house, located a quarter mile east of the railroad crossing, from 1940 unitl his death in 1975. (Courtesy of the Blue Ridge Institute)

something… just so that person would feel like he paid something. I never turned anyone down" ("Accent" 1E). He fails to mention in his list of modes of transport the small boat he had to use to cross the Smith River to get to an expectant mother in the middle of night in the 1930's (H. Mullins).

Dr. Green was an exceptional physician and for many years the only trained surgeon in the county. He is credited with stopping a local

Figure 6.   Dr. Green maintained a medical office in the building attached to the Ferrum Drug Company building from 1950's until the 1970's. (Courtesy of David Clements)

diphtheria epidemic in the 1930's by correctly diagnosing the disease and demanding that the state health department rush vaccine to the area. In the newspaper interview he pointedly criticized younger doctors for thinking they could only practice medicine in a hospital. He was always on call and went wherever he was needed whenever he was needed. Case in point, when my grandfather, Luther Smith (1872-1968), was shot in the arm while trying to break up a fight in his store, Dr. Green drove five miles to the store, staunched the bleeding, determined there were two bullet wounds (not one "through and through" wound as my grandfather apparently insisted), cleaned and dressed the wounds as store patrons watched in fascination. My grandfather lived another thirty years and enjoyed remarkably good health until his death at age 95.

Slone lists seven pharmacists: Ben Stone, W.H. Baxter, R.W. Simms, Myrtle Krouse, J.A. Moore, J.A. Vernon and E.J. Caton. The latter two men worked in drug stores operated by Mary Hurt Whitehead in the 1950's and 60's. Presumably the first named individuals worked in the drug store owned by J. K. Hurt. In the 1930's, J. A. Moore operated the

Figure 7.   The interior of the Ferrum Drug Company as it appeared in the early 1950's. Pictured from the left are Mary Hurt Whitehead, owner; E.J. Caton, pharmacist; and Bill Lemons, clerk. (Courtesy of the Blue Ridge Institute)

People's Pharmacy in the first Menefee Building, a two-story brick edifice located on the west side of the railroad crossing to the south of Hurt and Company. (see ch. 8, fig. 1) The building must have burned around 1939 before the devastating fire of March 1940 as there is no mention of the building in the newspaper coverage of the 1940 fire. Hugh and Shirley Green operated Green's Pharmacy from 1970 to 2003 on the corner where the original Bank of Ferrum was located. Mr. Green still volunteers as a part time pharmacist at the Tri-Area Community Clinic.

Slone lists three barbers: H.L. Maxey, V.A. Dodson, and Ted Boyd (P. Slone, Monogaph 14). Boyd's Barber Shop offered the usual haircuts and shaves with generous applications of talcum powder, hair tonic, and shaving lotion which the customer could choose from a variety of brands in tall bottles on a shelf under the wall mirror behind the barber's chair. Another service offered by Mr. Boyd to his customers was a hot shower. As late as the 1950's many homes did not have hot running water even if they did have cold running water. Boyd had a wood-fired hot water heater and a shower head in a room with a cement floor and drain that many a country boy availed himself of before going out with his girlfriend on a Saturday night. As the hot water tank was small and demand brisk,

Figure 8.   The Robert Skinnell house built in the 1890's. (Courtesy of the Blue Ridge Institute)

61

long showers were frowned upon.

Slone fails to note that two beauticians, Goldie Smith Edwards (1916-2000) and Era Whittaker (1916-1978), operated beauty shops in Ferrum in 1955. Edwards, in fact, according to Gladys Edwards Willis in *Goin' Up Shootin' Creek* had been the first professional beautician to open a beauty shop in Ferrum in the late 1930's and was a pioneer in the field for western Franklin County (43). In the 1960's, Keiko Young opened a third beauty shop at the foot of Nolen's Hill behind the bank. Other beauty salons have been operated in the village over the succeeding years. Like Wingfield before him Slone fails to mention Jack Menefee's Pool Room located adjacent to and south of Hurt and Company until he lists it as one of the businesses destroyed in the 1940 fire.

Slone notes that R.M. Young operated a small hotel on the west side of the railroad crossing and Berta Nolen Boothe operated a boarding house a few hundred yards east of the crossing (P. Slone, Monograph 13). The *Virginia Business Directory of 1917* lists another boarding house operated by Robert Skinnell which presumably would have been located

Figure 9.   The interior of the Ferrum Cafe from 1954 with the owner Dewey Nolen behind the counter. (Courtesy of the Blue Ridge Insititute)

in the large elegant four square house located on the hill at the south end of the trackside business block on Rte. 623 (Salmon 352). Known locally as the Skinnell house, the property in more recent times was converted into "The House" restaurant and subsequently has been severely damaged by fire.

Slone lists seven individuals who operated restaurants in Ferrum: M.S. Hollandsworth, Jack Menefee, Myrtle (Menefee) Bowles, J.M. Manor, Oscar (Mutt) Canaday, Dewey Nolen (P. Slone, Monograph 13). Jim Mullins in his diary from 1933 specifically mentions going to the Blue Haven Café in Ferrum which presumably was in the first Menefee Building. Colonel James Stanley remembered that on V-J Day in August of 1945 Mr. Manor moved the restaurant juke box out onto the sidewalk and that there was literally dancing in the street to celebrate the end of the Second World War.

Little seems to have been recorded about the mining engineers or the miners who produced the iron ore taken out of Flint/Summit Hill. The iron deposits discovered in 1889 by the Roanoke and Southern surveyors just a few hundred yards south of the station yielded a good commercially mineable grade of ore (Wingfield 26). In the early 1890's the Crozier Iron Works of Roanoke operated an iron mine here (Hurt, "History" 10). The president of the Iron Works was Colonel David Houston who also was an organizing officer of the railroad. The Brown Hill Mining Company of Ferrum was one of just four iron mines still operating in the county in 1897 (Salmon 346). Iron deposits dot the county and as early as the 1790's provided ore for the Carron Iron Works on Story Creek just a mile north of what would become Ferrum. Named for a famous Scottish iron works founded in Falkirk Scotland in 1759, the Carron furnace was owned and operated by Swinfield Hill, Walter Bernard, and William Armstrong. Not wanting competition to his larger Washington Iron Works on Furnace Creek in Rocky Mount, James Callaway bought the Carron Works in 1802 (Salmon 111-12). In the early 1890's, the Roanoke and Southern Railroad construction engineers used the large stones that had comprised the Carron iron furnace to build the piers for one of the rail bridges crossing Story Creek north of the village.

In 1946 some of the professional men, merchants and other civic minded citizens of the village organized the Ferrum Lion's Club. As an affiliate of Lion's Club International, the world's largest service organization, the local club adopted the goals of the group and dedicated itself to performing community service, to helping those in need, especially the visually challenged, and to encouraging personal and professional development and leadership skills. Seventy-three years later under the current leadership of David Newcombe the club still exists and continues to serve the community. Among those 1946 charter members were Kyle Goode, Luther Burnett, Sheriff Shively, Herman Shively, Guy Nolen, Buford Nolen, Jack Renick, Noan Shockley, Dr. J. M. Green, Buel Bowling, C.L. Ross, and Posey Ross. Though technically not a charter member because he joined a few months after the group organized, Edward Goode at age 91 is the longest serving member of the group (K. Goode).

Chapter 6

Neither Snow nor Rain: Village Post Offices

As previously noted, in 1888 George W. Turner opened a post office in his store near what is now the intersection of Rte. 40 and Turner's Creek Road (Rte. 748) one mile west of what was to become the village of Ferrum; he named the post office Sophronia in honor of his wife, the former Sophronia Luke (Drewery 74). When the store failed in 1891, Turner sought to move the Sophronia Post Office to Ferrum. The government decided rather to decommission the Sophronia Post Office and to open a new one named Ferrum with a new post master. A post office was opened in Ferrum in March of 1892. The first post master in Ferrum was Florence N. Menefee, wife of George A. Menefee who operated a store on the east side of the railroad crossing, and presumably he housed the post office in his store as was the custom of the time. A post office that had opened in 1877 at Pernello about three miles south west of Ferrum on Rte. 623 was closed and consolidated with the Ferrum Post Office in January, 1905 (Wingfield 226,228). Early in the twentieth century, a wood frame post office building was constructed, and this building served the community until the 1950's. (This historic building survives to this day; C. Buford Nolen bought it and moved it to a site near Philpott Lake to use as a hunting cabin.) The Ferrum Post Office was moved to the west side of the crossing in the mid-1950's and located in the "new" (after the 1940 fire) Menefee block at the south end of the trackside business district. In January of 1958 the post office was moved

Figure 1.   The first purpose built Ferrum Post Office was erected around 1914 adjacent to the Ferrum Supply Company, two hundred feet to the east of the railroad crossing. (Courtesy of the Blue Ridge Institute)

Figure 2.   This building housed the Ferrum Post Office from 1958 until the early 1980's and was located on Nolen's Hill Road, directly behind the drug store and first bank building. (Courtesy of the Blue Ridge Institute)

to a new masonry building constructed by Dr. J.M. Green on Nolen's Hill road behind the Ferrum Drug Company. Since the early 1980's, the post office has been housed in a modern brick building located on the east side of the crossing no more than one hundred yards from its original 1892 site.

From 1888 to September 1892 George W. Turner is listed as postmaster of the original Sophronia Post Office which as stated was very near the present village on the headwaters of Story Creek on the Pinckard settlement. Subsequent Ferrum postmasters and the beginning date of their service follow: Florence N. Menefee 10/03/1892; John W. Haynes 11/01/1893 (Mr. Haynes also was an early store owner perhaps in partnership with his brother Brooks Haynes; the Haynes family cemetery is on the northwest side of the village presumably near Haynes Knob); William L. Thornton 07/03/1897 (this man may be related to the Thornton family for whom Thornton Mountain a few miles to the east of the village is named, and more than likely he operated the store on the west side of the tracks shown on the N&W 1898 Engineering and Maintenance of Way drawing); George E. Goode 09/02/1899; H.

Figure 3.   The current Ferrum Post Office sits on a site just a few feet from the first Post Office in the George Menefee store and the 1914 Post Office. (Courtesy of the Blue Ridge Institute)

Eldridge Menefee 09/18/1899 (another prominent early store owner on the west side of the railroad tracks); Charles A. Hickman 02/23/1911(a business partner of H.E. Menefee); John O. Boothe 03/30/1914 (during Boothe's tenure the Ferrum Post Office moved permanently out of the stores and into its own small white frame building two-hundred feet east of the railroad crossing just off Rt. 40); Silas E. Corn 02/23/1918; Bertha Thompson 05/20/1922; Claude B. Nolen 07/19/1934; Veltie Austin Dodson 08/16/1944; Ruby Martin Nicholson Skinnell 02/01/1946 to 1978 (*Franklin County Post Offices Over the Years,* 20). More recent Ferrum Post Masters have included Joe Kitts, Richard Woods, Diane Durham, and Melissa Prillaman.

The Ferrum postal routes have remained essentially the same down through the years. Postal Route 1 followed the Prillaman Switch Road (Rte. 767), Hawpatch Road (Rte. 606), Waidsboro Road (Rte. 607), Skillet Road (757), Beech Mountain Road (Rte. 766), Rte. 40 back to Ferrum. Postal Route 2 included Old Ferrum Road (Rte. 864), the college, Ferrum Mountain Road (Rte. 602), Sawmill Road (Rte. 752), Thompson Ridge Road (Rte. 788), Fairy Stone Park Road (Rte. 623), Pernello Road(Rte. 781). Postal Route 3 leaves Ferrum on Ingramville Road (Rte. 623), Henry Road (Rte. 605), Franklin Street (Rte. 40) to Endicott. Some of the early rural route carriers were J.K. Hurt, George W. Wade, Thomas G. Ingram, William Curtis Brammer, Pedro T. Slone, John R. Buckner, Abel Mason, Kyle Goode, B.M. Bowling, Claude B. Nolen, and Naomi Nolen (P. Slone, Monograph 15). Later carriers included R. W. Akers and Daniel Quinn. Current carriers include Shane Boyd, Cindy Scott, and Tracy Meade.

Chapter 7

School Days: Elementary, Secondary, and College

A public school was built for the village soon after the post office and railroad station opened. Frank Hurt states that a three-room frame building was erected in 1894 across the hill from the Elkenney (Elkanah) Keys estate west of the railroad and served the community until 1907 (24). Pedro Slone describes the first school as "a two-story, two-roomed frame building" that stood on the hill north of the Keys home and served the community until it was razed in 1911 and rebuilt on the present school grounds (P. Slone, Monograph 8). A 1917 deed shows H.L. Poff and Rufus Ferguson sold property in Ferrum to Mead Hollandsworth and clearly states that a portion of this land had previously belonged to the county and had been the site of the Ferrum School. A 1942 deed records that Hollandsworth sold this land and improvements to Claire and Elma Young. The site of the 1894 Ferrum School was therefore on the hill directly west of the railroad crossing near the Claire Young house (*see ch. 12, fig. 10*) which is now owned by Darnell Young Green.

Slone's reference to "present" school grounds is to the property opposite Saint James Methodist Church bought by the county November 6, 1911, from J.O. and Berta Boothe (formerly Nolen). *Franklin County Deed Book # 60*, page 321 describes this lot as bordering on the corner of D.A. Nicholson's property and containing one acre. Franklin County built a new school on this site around 1915 when some of the public

Figure 1.   This 1925 photograph depicts the Ferrum School that was built circa 1915 on land purchased from John and Berta Boothe in 1911. (Courtesy of the Library of Virginia)

school students were moved there from a building on the Ferrum Training School campus. A photograph dated July 10, 1925, from the Archives of the Library of Virginia (School Building Services Photograph Collection) depicts Ferrum School as a two-story, two-room frame building replete with bell cupola. Photographs of the main street of Ferrum in the 1920's clearly show this building indeed standing in the distance on the "present"

Figure 2.   This three room structure was built in 1928 after fire destroyed the 1915 school building and served Ferrum students until 1964. (Franklin County High School Yearbook - The Animo 1986)

school grounds (*see ch. 7, fig. 10*).

Prior to 1928 this building burned and Ferrum students in grades one to seven were allowed to use a building on the Ferrum Training School campus until a new school could be rebuilt on the same site (P. Slone, Monograph 8). A Survey of Public School Plants from the Virginia Department of Education from 1936 shows that a frame three-room school building housing grades one to seven was constructed in 1928 at a cost of $4,000. A July 1937 National Fire Insurance Inspection and Survey Report describes this building as a one-story frame building on a brick foundation with a metal roof; the building consisted of three classrooms lighted by electricity and heated by stoves. Two of the classrooms were divided by folding doors that could be opened to create a large meeting room for school or community use. This building was in use until 1963 when a modern brick elementary school was constructed west of the village off Rte. 40.

Some of the first teachers in the original school included Mrs. Minnie Goode, Mrs. Emma Goode, T.A. Walker, Miss Mattie Wade, D.A. Nicholson, and J.O. Boothe (P. Slone, Monograph 8). Though Mr. Pedro Slone never taught in Ferrum, he did teach in at least four schools in the neighboring Long Branch and Blackwater districts. Some of his contracts with the county school board stipulated that he would be paid "when the money was in the treasury." His monthly salaries varied from a low of $18 to a high of $27.50 per month during his tenure as a teacher from 1899 to 1908 (Ramsey, "Profiles"). As if the demands of a teaching job were not challenging enough, a 1905 contract between the Board of School Trustees of the Blackwater School District and one Laura Montgomery required her to make or cause to be made the fires and to sweep or cause to be swept the school house floor. And to add insult to injury, she was required to furnish "fuel, brooms and ax" for the school! (*Callaway of Yesterday* 19).

Ferrum elementary school teachers in the 1940's included : Edna Hash Whitlock Booth, Eva Bowling , Arline Brammer, Mignon Brammer, Helen Corn, Essie Nicholson Easter, Mae R. Fulcher, Elmer Hum, Minnie Cooper Jefferson, Geneva T. Johnson, Ruth Hash Jones, Mamie Dudley King, Betty Ingram Mathews, Blanche Pinckard, Myrtle

Figure 3.   The new Ferrum Elementary School was built in 1964. (Courtesy of the Blue Ridge Institute)

Pinckard, Lera Bennett Smith, Annie Stanley, and Mildred Via.

Since the opening in 1964 of the modern brick elementary school off Rte. 40 west of the village, another cadre of dedicated faculty and staff has served the children of Ferrum. Among the longer serving individuals are the following administrators, teachers and staff:

Principals :

K. Edward Goode	Christopher Corallo	Linda Fisher
Col. Alfred Divers	Sandra Ruff	Marcie Altice
Larry Meadors	Gwen Adkins	Jennifer Prillaman Talley

Teachers:

Ruth Jones	Emma Wright	Bettie Baber
Macie Woods	Glenda Scott Thompson	Sandra Grant
Billie Corn	Evelyn Patterson Dowdy	Janice Camenish
Kaye Linnane	Mary Jane Lynch	Mary Richardson
Anne Campbell	Gertrude Hickin Sigmon	Becky Newbill
Ann Cardwell	Mandy Guilliams Brown	Thomas Young
Florella Johnson	Natalie Quesenberry	Fannie Gentry
Gloria Rabon	Diane Johnson Shively	Judy Thompson
Betty Corvin	Robin Bowling Whitmer	Tressa Moore
Evelyn Hobbes	Sarah Cundiff Bowles	Amanda Meade
Doris Fitzgerald	Johnnie Mae Shields	Valerie Brown
Anne Tyler	Betty Gruver	Joyce Howell

School Secretaries:

Shirley Dodson Wright   Regena Bussey   Freda Mullins

Cafeteria Managers:

Frances Buckner   Marie Johnson   Shirley Thompson

Claudine Radford   Elizabeth Kennedy

In 1913 the Women's Missionary Society and the Virginia Annual Conference of the Methodist Episcopal Church decided to build a modern boarding school for under-served mountain children on a site less than one half mile from the village. Ferrum Training School under the leadership of Dr. Benjamin Moore Beckham was destined to enhance the prosperity and the cultural life of the village. Recognizing the value of having such a school in their midst, enlightened members of the small community raised over $1,500 to help fund the project. Hurt lists the following individuals who donated money in amounts varying from $5 to $200 (22):

D.A. Nicholson	W.H. Buckner	C.A. Hickman
G.A Menefee	R.L. Ferguson	C.M. Burnett
J.R. Buckner	J.C. Jamison	P.T. Slone
T.C. Nicholson	C.H. Hodges	R.B. Skinnell
A.L. Lemons	M.O. Lemons	E.M. Young
W.P. Hash	J.K. Hurt	I.T. Cannaday
W.T. Ingram	J.R. Shively	F.F. Turner
J.R.L. Woods	H.E. Menefee	J.J. Brammer
	P.M. Ingram	

Acquisition of land for the school began in 1913 with the purchase of eighty acres by the Ferrum Board of Trustees from George Goode for $3,700. The original academic and residential buildings stand on this site as do most of the current campus structures. Also in 1913, the Board purchased fifty acres at the foot of Saul's Knob (Ferrum Mountain) from Meade Hollandsworth for $1,000 . This property contained a strong spring and sufficient fall in elevation to supply the school with a reliable source of water (Hurt, *History* 30). The Board completed the original purchase of property in 1916 when it bought ninety-six acres from Rev.

*Figure 4.   Dr. Benjamin Moore Beckham (1868-1957) was
instrumental in the founding of Ferrum Training School and served
as its president from 1913 to 1934. (Courtsey of the Blue Ridge
Institute)*

Thomas Page Duke and Jennie Ward Duke for $8,000. This farm was part of the Sam and Julia Ward Estate and is now the site of residential halls, the Blue Ridge Institute, and Adams Lake (Hurt, *History* 51). Since 1916, Ferrum College has continued to acquire property in and around the village and now owns over 700 acres.

The Blue Ridge Institute, founded in 1972 by M.G. Goodpasture and others, offers a good example of the salutary influence of the college on the community and confirmation of the foresight of the village leaders in 1913. The collection of artifacts of Appalachian culture amassed by the staff of the BRI led by Roddy Moore is remarkable with its living history centerpiece the Blue Ridge Farm Museum. Thousands of visitors descend on Ferrum on the fourth Saturday of October each year to attend the Institute's annual Blue Ridge Folklife Festival. They see live demonstrations of Appalachian crafts and skills, listen to authentic mountain music, and

Figure 5.   The Blue Ridge Institute and Museum building was constructed in 1986. (Courtesy of the Blue Ridge Institute)

sample traditional foods prepared on open fires or on wood stoves.

While the influence of Ferrum Training School (1914-1940), Ferrum Junior College (1940-1971), Ferrum College (1971-Present) on the life of the village cannot be over-estimated, others, including most notably Dr. Frank Benjamin Hurt (son of John Kemper Hurt and Lelia Angle

Figure 6.   A circa 1928 view of the Ferrum Training School campus. (Courtesy of the Blue Ridge Institute)

Hurt), have written extensively about the history of the college. Their works, especially Hurt's 1977 *A History of Ferrum College*, contain a wealth of information about the antecedents of this venerable learning institution. A final word, however, about Ferrum College, and this is not meant in any way to take anything from or to minimize the work of the numerous men and women who have labored through the years since Dr. Beckham's original struggle to found and to sustain the Training School. But few would dispute that had it not been for the tireless work of C. Ralph Arthur in the 1950's, there is little doubt that the college would have closed its doors. Those with knowledge of the serious challenges faced by the college at this time credit Dr. Arthur with almost single-handedly saving the then struggling Junior College and laying the ground work for a remarkable transformation and another sixty years of service to thousands of Ferrum students.

Perhaps because of the presence of Ferrum Training School within a mile of the village or possibly because of the excellent passenger train service permitting students who could afford the train fare to attend the public Henry High School, Ferrum was the last community of its size in the county to receive a public high school. In 1940, Franklin County constructed at a cost of $19,000 a two-story brick building with coal-

Figure 7.   Ferrum High School was built in 1940 and functioned as a high school until 1950. (Courtesy of the Blue Ridge Institute)

80

Figure 8.   Beverly Ingram is pictured by an early school bus.
He drove a school bus transporting students who lived in the Ferrum
area for over forty years. (Franklin County High School Yearbook -
The Animo 1986)

fired central heating housing six classrooms, modern restrooms, a cafeteria, library and a principal's office. Two of the upstairs class rooms were divided by floor to ceiling folding doors which could be opened to create a large multi-purpose room or community meeting space. About 1950, two additional classrooms were added; these rooms were equipped with restrooms and designed to serve first and second graders. Prior to 1940, Ferrum students wishing to go to a public high school had to go to Rocky Mount, Henry, or Callaway. Rocky Mount built its first high school in the early 1900's, and in 1924 the town built an accredited, modern brick high school "...equipped with sanitary drinking fountains, gymnasium, and cafeteria" (Claiborne 25). The Henry community opened a junior high school in 1917 and a high school in 1929 (E. Goode). According to Lizzie C. Robertson, a former principal, the Class of 1929 was the first graduating class from the four-year high school at Callaway (Robertson 9). As roads were poor and school bus service limited, students desiring to go beyond the seventh grade had few choices, and for the vast majority formal schooling ended with elementary school. School bus transportation in Franklin County began in 1926 with a single bus serving the Sontag area; in 1935 only about 25% of county

Figure 9.   Edward Goode served as a Ferrum High School teacher and Ferrum School principal for more than thirty years. (Ferrum School Photo Album)

students were transported to school by bus (Hartlely 291).

Though never accredited as a college preparatory school, Ferrum High School offered a high school diploma until it was consolidated with all the other county high schools into Franklin County High School in 1951. A junior high school program for grades eight and nine continued until Franklin County Junior High School opened in 1964. After this building ceased to be used as a public school, it was acquired by Ferrum College in 1972 and became the first home of the Blue Ridge Institute.

Ferrum High School teachers and subjects taught from 1940 to 1951:

1940-41:William Ingram, Principal, Science; Horace A. Bragg, Math and History; Betty Dean, English and French

1941-42: Jack Renick, Principal, French and History; Elmer Hum, Math and Science; Elizabeth Carroll, English and History

1942-43: Jack Renick, Principal, French and History; Lera B. Smith, English and History; Virginia Carroll, Science and English; Martha McGhee, English and History

1943-44: Jack Renick, Principal, and Science; Louise E. Shriver,

Home Economics and History; Olivia Newbill, Math and Science

1944-45: Lucille Dudley Thomas, Principal, Science and French; Louise Pearson Cobbs, English; Gustava Hash, Math; Mignon Brammer, English and History

1945-46: A.C. Robertson, Principal and Science; Louise P. Cobbs, English and Math; Mignon Brammer, English and History; Lera B. Smith, Science and History

1946-47: Noan Shockley, Principal and Math; Louise P. Cobbs, English; Lera B. Smith, History and Science; Edward Goode, Math and Science

1947-48: Noan Shockley, Principal and Math; Louise P. Cobbs, English; Lera B. Smith, History and Science; Edward Goode, Math and Science; Mignon Brammer, English and History

1948-49: Noan Shockley, Principal and Science; Edward Goode, Math and Science; Louise P. Cobbs, English; Flora Morris, History and Government; Lera B. Smith, Librarian and History

1949-50: Noan Shockley, Principal and Math; Edward Goode, Math; Lera B. Smith, History and English; Louise P. Cobbs, English and History; Mrs. L.P. Jackson, English, Science, and History

1950-51: Noan Shockley, Principal; Edward Goode, Math; Louise P. Cobbs, Civics, English and History; Charles E. Brauer, English, Biology and History; Evelyn A. Terry, Science, English, and History

(Staff rosters for Ferrum High School 1940-1951 were copied from the *Ferrum High School 1942-1951 Reunion Program Booklet* from 1992 loaned by Lloyd Edwards-Class of 1944.)

The village never had a school for Black children. A hand drawn map of Franklin County Schools from the early 1920's shows no schools for Black children in the entire Brown Hill District which included Ferrum. The Survey of Public School Plants cited earlier shows three one-room Black elementary schools within a few miles of Ferrum for the school sessions 1938 through 1944. The survey map shows Rockfield School (built in 1905) to the west off Rte. 40 between Ferrum Mountain Road (Rte. 602) and Turner's Creek Road (Rte.748) (This location for

Rockfield, however, could be an error as no Black children were known to live within two to three miles of that area. A more likely site would be between Rte. 40 and Rte. 623 off King Richard Road near Rock Spring Church.) Smith's School (built in 1930 with Rosenwald funds) was located to the east on Beech Mountain Road (Rte. 767), and Cooks Knob School (built in 1929) was still farther to the east off Six Mile Post Road (Rte. 640). These schools offered grades 1-7 and had enrollments varying from a low of twelve students to a high of twenty-five. The only high school program for Blacks began in 1926 in Rocky Mount (Hartley 288). The one-room Rockfield School was built in 1905 at a cost of $400, but in the 1938-1944 Survey it was valued at only $50 indicating what can only be described as a dilapidated condition. The question of separate but equal raises itself.

In his "Personal Reflections" Dr. Harold W. Ramsey, Franklin County Superintendent of Schools from 1927 to 1968, wrote " …it was apparent that while the school system operated under the laws of the state requiring separate and equal facilities, this was only a half truth. They were separate but obviously not equal to the schools for white students" (Ramsey, "Reflections"). Dr. Ramsey and the school board began making serious improvements to the Black schools in 1949 with the building of a modern brick building on the grounds of the Franklin County Training School in Rocky Mount. By the 1950's Black children of all school ages (6 to 18) in the Ferrum area were bussed to this school which in 1957 was renamed the Lee M. Waid School after a prominent Black Rocky Mount business man and proponent of better education for Black children. All public schools in Franklin County were fully integrated largely without incident in 1970 sixteen years after the Supreme Court Brown v. Board of Education decision outlawing public school segregation.

No doubt early schooling would have stressed the basics of reading, writing and arithmetic, but by the 1920's the curriculum was more sophisticated. A *Virginia Record for Class Grades* for the school-year 1926-27 for seventh grade students at Sontag (and presumably at Ferrum as well) lists grades for Deportment, Reading, Spelling, Writing (Pensmanship), Mathematics, History, Civics, Hygiene (Health), Physical Education, Drawing, and Agriculture. By the 1950's weekly music, art, and even religion classes were offered. With the launch of the Russian satellite Sputnik in 1957, the School Board deemed it wise to add Science to the elementary curriculum and spanking new science textbooks began arriving in the schools midyear. Little or no provision was made for special needs students until federal funds became available to support Special Education classes in the mid-1960's (Hartley 298, 302). It should be noted that while some special needs children were banned by law from public schools, e.g., blind, deaf, mentally retarded, emotionally disturbed children, a few special needs children including physically disabled and some Down Syndrome children were allowed to attend the public schools. The passage in 1975 of *U.S. Public Law 94-142*, the Education of All Handicapped Children Act, greatly expanded the rights of all children with disabilities.

For many years the Circuit Court Judge appointed a three-person School Electoral Board who in turn appointed individuals to represent the magisterial districts on the Franklin County School Board. In the 1980's the county began electing School Board members. Some of the citizens who have served either as appointed or elected members of the School Board representing the Ferrum area include: D.A. Nicholson, P. M. Ingram, J.W. Wade, Posey Ross, Claire Young, Shirley Young Green, Kathlene Holt, Carl Dudley, and Julie McBride Nix, who is the current

Figure 10.   In this early view of Ferrum looking to the east, the 1915 Ferrum School building can be clearly seen. (Courtesy of the Blue Ridge Institute)

chairperson of the board.

While the School Board selects a superintendent to administer the school system, establishes policies and prepares a multi-million dollar school system budget, it has no control over the raising of taxes or the actual appropriation of funds for the schools. The elected Board of Supervisors, as part of it governing responsibilities, controls all county revenues. Through the years the Ferrum community has been represented on the Franklin County Board of Supervisors by Harry Bryant, Sheriff Shively, Luther Burnett, Thurmond Scott, Jack Martin, Ronnie Woods, Hubert Quinn, Bobby Thompson and Tim Tatum.

Chapter 8

Fire!

While the Ferrum schools suffered just the one fire in the 1920's, other village structures were lost to fire on a regular basis. Over the years fire destroyed the stave mill, the first Menefee brick store, the Brooks Haynes Shop, the R.H. Young Hotel, the insulator pin and bracket mill, and private residences. No fire, however, was as devastating as the conflagration that occurred in the spring of 1940. Pedro Slone lists the businesses destroyed in the March 21, 1940, fire as C.A. Hickman's Store, the Restaurant, Pool Room, Barber Shop, the J.K. Hurt General Merchandise Store, Hurt Hardware Store, Hurt Drug Store, Hurt Wholesale Feed Store. He omits the Beauty Shop and the Telephone Exchange among others (P. Slone, Monograph 15-16).

Myrtle Menefee Bowles (daughter of H.E. Menefee) recalled in a Jan. 1, 1986, *Franklin News-Post* article about the fire that eleven businesses burned: Veltie Dodson's barber shop, the Ferrum Café, a music shop, Jack Menefee's pool room, the Ferrum Jewelry Store, the Mutual Telephone Exchange, Goldie Edwards' and Irene Brammer's Ferrum Beauty Shop, the Menefee Radio shop, Hurt and Company Hardware, Hurt and Company Grocery and Drygoods Store, and Ferrum Drug Company. In the same article, however, she further mentions other businesses lost in the fire including her mother Lew Angle Menefee's casket and shroud business; the Hickman General Merchandise Store;

the medical office of Dr. J. M. Green; and several buildings that her mother rented out to other business men. Mrs. Bowles also failed to mention the several residential apartments located on the second floors of both the Hurt and Hickman buildings. No doubt, the occupants of these apartments lost all of their worldly possessions as well. It was speculated at the time that the fire originated in one of these apartments, but no official cause for this destructive fire was ever established.

The March 22, 1940, *Roanoke Times* headlined the fire on the front page and reported that eleven buildings (not eleven businesses) burned in less than three hours sending flames high enough to be seen ten miles away. The *Times* quoted Ben Corn, Assistant Cashier of the Ferrum Bank, as estimating the monetary loss at $250,000 with little of that loss covered by insurance. Even

Figure 1.   The first brick Menefee building shown here on the left was destroyed by fire prior to the 1940 fire. (Courtesy of the V.A. Dodson Family)

allowing for the difference in 1940 dollars and today's dollars (which would place the loss at more than four million dollars), the estimate seems low. In 1986, Frank Hurt, son of J. K. Hurt who founded many of the destroyed businesses, observed "the fire wiped out much of the capital of Ferrum; … (it) didn't wipe out all of the buildings, but it got most of them" (Franklin County Historical Society). Even attempts to save some of the merchandise and equipment from the doomed businesses were in vain. At some risk to themselves, well-intentioned people placed these salvaged goods along the railroad tracks at what they thought would be a safe distance from the flames, but the intense heat from the fire ignited

Figure 2. The front page of The Roanoke Times on March 22, 1940, carried the news of the calamitous fire that nearly destroyed the village. (Courtesy of the Virginia Room of the Roanoke City Public Library)

Figure 3. Onlookers survey the ruins of the J.K. Hurt and Company. (Courtesy of the Blue Ridge Institute)

and destroyed most of these items as well.

The *Roanoke Times* in its coverage of the fire went so far as to list what was, in fact, left of Ferrum: "several service stations, Ferrum Junior College, the post office, the Norfolk and Western station, a store, a mercantile concern, the Chevrolet garage, and the Ferrum Veneer Company." The newspaper fails to list the First National Bank as surviving the fire, perhaps because it did suffer some damage.

The 1940 fire would have undoubtedly destroyed the entire village and perhaps cost several lives had not some quick-witted volunteers sprung into action. The 1929 Seagrave fire engine from Rocky Mount carried only enough water to prime its pump and therefore had to have a separate source of water. There were no fire hydrants in Ferrum, and the flow of water in the small stream that flowed through the village was insufficient to pump. Someone realized that if the stream were blocked, enough water would collect behind the makeshift dam to allow the fire engine to pump a continuous stream of water onto the fire and onto the

Figure 4.   This photograph shows the fully restored 1929 Seagrave Special Fire Engine. (Courtesy of the Rocky Mount Volunteer Fire Department)

buildings not yet ablaze. Using sacks of feed and beans from the doomed Hurt warehouse, volunteers constructed a dam which provided the firemen with sufficient water to prevent the fire from spreading to the north end of the village and more importantly to the thousands of gallons of gasoline in storage tanks beside Young's Garage. Sometime after the fire, a wheel operated sluice gate was installed at the bridge crossing the stream so that the water could be dammed if the need ever arose again (Young). (The 1929 Seagrave fire engine used by the Rocky Mount firemen that night has been fully restored by the Rocky Mount Fire Department and is proudly displayed in the North Main Street Fire Station.)

All of the businesses, an estimated twenty in all, and an unknown number of apartments to the south of the First National Bank of Ferrum were destroyed. Some have lamented that Ferrum was never the same after this calamitous fire. And it is true that many of the businesses were never able to rebuild. One enterprise in particular was devastated. Of the large complex that had been Hurt and Company including the recently (1930) refurbished main store building with its handsome brick façade, nothing south of the First National Bank survived. Some years later, Mary Hurt Whitehead, daughter of J.K. Hurt, built a single story brick building to house the Ferrum Drug Company and a doctor's office on the

*Figure 5.   The 1950's Ferrum Drug Company building as it
appeared in 2019. (Courtesy of the Blue Ridge Institute)*

site of her father's brick building.

The last major fire in the village occurred in the mid 1960's. This fire completely destroyed the paint and auto body shop of Ferrum Garage. Consumed also by the flames was a large, old warehouse that had once served Ferrum Mercantile and the earlier Ferrum Supply Company. Both of these structures were located behind the Garage and Mercantile buildings along Rte. 767, the Prillaman Switch Road. It soon became apparent that the newly-organized Ferrum Volunteer Fire Department, even with the aid of other local fire departments, was no match for this fire. Many onlookers present remembered all too well the disastrous fire of 1940 and were horrified by the prospect that history was in danger of repeating itself. Fortunately, two very large Bassett Fire Department pumper trucks arrived and quickly had the flames under control. Of course, these powerful fire engines had been bought for the expressed purpose of controlling potential large fires in the town of Bassett's furniture factories. No doubt, the foresight of the citizens of Bassett saved the village of Ferrum from another devastating loss to its old enemy fire.

Chapter 9

Bring Out Your Dead

Myrtle Menefee Bowles in her 1986 interview with the *Franklin News-Post* about the 1940 fire recalled that her mother, Lew Angle Menefee, lost her coffin and shroud business to the fire. J.K. Hurt and Company also sold coffins and shrouds, but that business ended with the fire. Mrs. Menefee , widow of H.E. Menefee, was by the standards of the time wealthy, and she not only re-established her mortuary business quickly, she also built a brick-fronted commercial building with four rental store fronts on the south end of the village at a cost of $25,000 (J. Stanley, interview). At this time in the early 1940's country people were still "shrouding" and burying their own dead. A shroud by definition is the cloth used to wrap a dead body, but in practice it came to refer to both the clothing placed on a body and the act of preparing or "laying out" of the corpse including the washing, combing of the hair, shaving, and dressing of the deceased. Interestingly, those who could afford it purchased new burial clothes for their loved ones, hence the shroud business. Often neighbors came to assist the grieving family with the painful but necessary ritual of shrouding the dead.

Of course coffins could be and were handmade, but a local coffin maker would need several days or more notice to make a fine six-sided steam curved wood coffin with a shellacked and varnished finish. The prudent with the means pre-planned and ordered fine hand-crafted coffins well in advance of their demise. Ordinary folks in the days before embalming was common practice, buried their dead within a day or two of death, especially in hot weather. As a consequence families often had to resort to store bought coffins. Ruby Woods Worley, long time Ferrum resident, recalled the tragic accidental death of a brother in the 1930's. Though only a small child at the time, she remembers accompanying her mother to buy a coffin from Mrs. Menefee. When the coffin arrived, they had to pass it through an open window to get it into and later, out of, the house.

In the first decade of the twentieth century, records show that a simple handmade coffin could be bought for as little as $2.25, and an inexpensive store-bought coffin could be purchased for as little as $3.15. A "homemade" coffin was usually just a simple pine box; sometimes painted, sometimes not, but more often covered with black muslin. Bought coffins depending on price varied in quality. An invoice from the Hickman and Menefee store in the 1920's described a coffin shipped by rail to Ferrum from the Burlington (N.C.) Coffin Company as "covered in white lambskin with white interior" (Franklin County Historical Society Collection).

Mrs. Lew Angle Menefee (1883-1969) was a canny businesswoman and is reputed to have bought her own coffin wholesale while she was still in the shroud and coffin business and before she was effectively forced out of business by the newfangled funeral homes. When she closed the business, she moved the coffin to an unused bedroom in her home to await the day it would be needed. The Rocky Mount funeral directors may have put her out of business, but she had the satisfaction of knowing that they would not be selling her family an overpriced casket upon her demise.

Usually, families buried their dead in graveyards located on family land with the head of the grave and the marker facing east toward the rising sun. Pedro Slone listed in 1955 no fewer than twenty-one burial places within a square mile of Ferrum:

> On the southwest side of the village, we have the Carter, Buckner, Ferguson and Rakes cemeteries. Nearer the railroad are the Keys graves and above the Summit Cut the Turners (colored) graves.

On the northwest are the Pinkard, Ward, Feasell, Haynes, Saul, F.J.C. Campus (Note: There were three graves on the west side of Schoolfield Chapel that since have been relocated), Hurts, Cousens, Beckner, Young, Shively and Angle cemeteries. On the east are the Menefee, St James Church, Angle-Young and Ingram cemeteries (P. Slone, Monograph 16).

As noted previously, the Saint James Church cemetery, though available since 1896-1897, was not much used until the 1930's.

Figure 1.   The burial of Mary Blankenship, infant daughter of Cora and Kenton Blankenship, in 1927 in the Saint James Cemetery. (Courtesy of the Blue Ridge Institute with permission of Charles Blankenship)

The protocol for burial in family cemeteries varied from family to family. For some, family meant immediate family only; others were more inclusive allowing servants, friends, in-laws, even pets to be buried in the plot. The Nolen family has an interesting story about their family graveyard which now lies on a hill overlooking the Ferrum College Campus. C.B. Nolen, Jr. and C.B. Nolen, III, confirmed the details. At the turn of the twentieth century, Berta Saul Nolen operated a boarding house just east of the Ferrum Railroad Station. One November evening, a Mr. Robinette arrived at her door seeking a meal and a night's lodging. Businessmen and salesmen who traveled to Ferrum by rail found the Nolen establishment both convenient and convivial. But this particular guest did the unthinkable and repaid Mrs. Nolen's hospitality by having the poor manners to die in his sleep in one of her rooms. To make matters worse, much worse, no one could locate any relatives to claim the body. It fell then to Mrs. Nolen to make arrangements for the unfortunate man. And so it was that in November of 1901, Mr. W. H. Robinette, a total stranger from only God knew where, was taken to Mrs. Nolen's family plot, and given a Christian burial outside the cemetery fence. Charity only extends so far after all.

The story, however, does not end there. A century or so later, a Ferrum

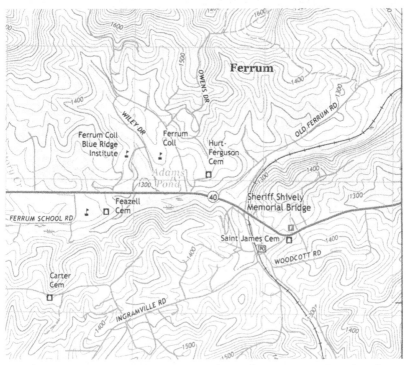

Figure 2. *A 2016 U.S. Geological Survey topographical map shows the location of some of the family cemeteries in or near Ferrum.*

100

College grounds crew accidentally tore down some of the cemetery fence. When they replaced the fence, naturally they assumed all the graves belonged inside the fence. Today, Mr. Robinette rests quietly among the Sauls and the Nolens including Mrs. Berta herself.

One last, but admittedly eerie, story remains to be told about the local practices and customs associated with death prior to the 1950's when professional morticians and funeral homes essentially removed the care of the dead from the purview of the family. As has been noted, embalming ended the necessity for speedy burials. Embalming, for all practical purposes, also ended the very real fear of being buried while still alive. In fact, the wake or the practice of "sitting up" with the dead was originally intended to watch for any signs of life lest the impending burial be premature.

My grandfather, Luther Smith, no mean spinner of tales, always grew grimly serious when he recounted this particular story worthy of Edgar Allen Poe himself. When a close neighbor died, my grandfather was called upon to help with the shrouding. He obliged and did what was called for including helping with the placing of the body into the coffin. The wake, the funeral and the burial proceeded without incident. Yet, for days and weeks after this funeral something nagged at him about this death and this burial; something vague, indefinite, undefined persisted in his memory far beyond grief, an emotion he knew well enough having lost many loved ones even two of his own children. Finally, he realized what had been bothering, even haunting, him these many days. When he had placed his hands under the body of his friend and neighbor to help lift him into the coffin, his back and the bed he lay on were warm to the touch. My grandfather went to his own grave absolutely convinced he had helped to bury a man alive.

Chapter 10

The Twentieth Century Arrives...Finally

When the 1940 fire nearly destroyed the whole village, the need for a reliable source of water could not have been made clearer. But it was not until 1968/1969 that the Ferrum Water and Sewage Authority (FWSA) was formed to serve both the village and Ferrum College. Before that time individual property owners used natural springs, hand-dug wells, and drilled wells to supply all their water needs. Septic tanks and drainage fields were the only modern sewage disposal systems available. Well into the 1960's, some people were still using outhouses and in most cases directing household waste water from washing clothes and bathing into ditches and even streams. The Ferrum Water and Sewage Authority was initiated by Ferrum College officials but supported by the community. G. Claire Young, Clyde Seeley, W.W. Burnett, Dr. C. Ralph Arthur, and Guy W. Nolen served as the first Board of Directors of the FWSA. A Farmers Home Administration grant paid for the original system that tapped into deep wells for fresh water and treated waste in a modern sewage treatment plant built on Rte. 864 north of the village. The college, businesses, and individuals had to pay connection fees and then pay monthly fees to maintain the system. Today, the system extends out to about a three-mile perimeter from the village center and serves an estimated 1,825 people. The system has a storage capacity of 600,000 gallons of water with about 140,000 gallons of usage per day ("County

Figure 1.   The Ferrum Fire Station stands on the site of the 1915 and 1928 Ferrum School Buildings. (Courtesy of the Blue Ridge Institute)

Figure 2.   The Ferrum Rescue Squad building was opened in 1996. (Courtesy of the Blue Ridge Institute)

Utilities").

In 1959, Ferrum College secured a well-used military surplus fire truck and local men refurbished and outfitted the vehicle. Thus was born the Ferrum Volunteer Fire Department which today is a modern, well-equipped department with twenty-five well-trained volunteers protecting eighty square miles. G. L. Martin, Jr. was the first Fire Chief and some of the original organizers included C. Ralph Arthur, Edward Goode, Bill Burnett, G. M. Holsclaw, John DeHart, Cleonard Whitlock, Bobby Shively, Des Hale, Mike Minucci, and Bal Edwards. The department is now housed in a brick, five-bay fire station that was built in the mid 1960's across from Saint James Church on the old elementary school grounds. In 1977, local citizens organized the Ferrum Volunteer Rescue Squad to answer another pressing community need for emergency services. The first Squad Captain was Donald Handy, and among the original volunteers were Charles Wagoner, Bobby Shively, Seneca Foote, James Shively, Ricky Boyd, Wayne Shively, Ron Stevens, and R. W. Akers. Since 1996, the squad has operated from a modern building on Route 40 one half mile east of the village. Housing ambulances and a crash truck, the three-bay building also now provides sleeping quarters for highly trained EMT's who are on call twenty-four hours a day. Combined, these two departments answer hundreds of calls each year.

A 1932-1933 *Virginia Highway Map* and Pedro Slone's 1955 description of early roads around Ferrum together provide an idea of the often shifting and confusing network of roads that served, and in some cases continue to serve, the village. The 1932-1933 map shows that State Route 40 (previously Rte. 20) was hard surfaced from the Pittsylvania County line to Rocky Mount, but from there westward to Ferrum and to the Patrick County line it was an improved Primary Highway of "Soil, Gravel, Sand, Clay." (Note: At this time Federal Highway 311- today's U.S. 220- was paved from the Henry County line to the Roanoke County line.) In the Ferrum area State Route 120 (present Rte. 602- Ferrum Mountain Road) is shown as an unimproved Primary Highway. Slone states that today's Prillaman Switch Road (Rte. 767) "...came from the south through Ferrum, led northwest by Ferrum Junior College through the gap in Saul's Knob (Ferrum Mountain) by way of Bleak Hill Farm to Callaway" (P. Slone, Monograph 5). Why state Rte. 120 would be classified as a Primary Highway and maintained as such is probably explained by the commercial interests on the other side of Ferrum Mountain (Saul's Knob) in Callaway. As early as 1914, Bleak Hill Farm was a Grade A Dairy and shipping milk by rail from Ferrum to Clover Creamery in Roanoke (Salmon 374); Algoma Orchards in Callaway would have also shipped apples from Ferrum. Of course, materials and merchandise made their way over the mountain from the Ferrum railroad station and businesses to Callaway. In 1921 the bricks used to build the Callaway School were shipped to Ferrum by rail and hauled over the mountain on old Rte. 120 by horse drawn wagons (*Callaway of Yesterday* 96).

On the map, Rte. 623 leading southwest to the Patrick County line is shown as an improved (soil, gravel, sand and clay) secondary road. All of the other roads in the area were unimproved secondary roads which in rainy weather often would have been impassable. Between Rte. 623 and present-day Rte. 40, Rte. 781 ran more or less parallel to Rte. 40 and before the 1930's served as the principal road leading west to Long Branch and Endicott. Today Pernello Road and King Richard Road follow this old road to within a mile of Ferrum. Another unimproved road Rte. 782 (today's Rte. 865-Timberline Road) is shown on the map coming into Ferrum from the southwest and proceeding through the village on the west side of the railroad tracks and then paralleling the tracks northeast toward Rocky Mount following the present Rte. 864-Old Ferrum Road. Slone describes a road "as entering Ferrum about where the present Veneer Plant is located and passing on out south of Saint James Church" (P. Slone, Monograph 4). The Veneer Plant was located about 300 yards south of the present railroad crossing, and before the coming of the railroad in the 1890's this road would have crossed Rte.767 (Prillaman Switch Road) south of the village and proceeded northeast toward Rocky Mount. An aerial photograph from 1937 clearly shows the remnants of this road which links with Rte.40 about one half mile east of Ferrum. Evidence exists of a road bed on the south side of present Rte. 40 leading east from the village. This old road bed and the older road Slone places "south of Saint James Church" may be evidence of the Brown Hill Turnpike which ran from the east through Ferrum toward Nicholas Creek and the Smith (Irvine) River. Ludwig Von

106

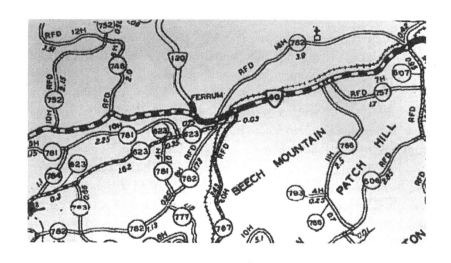

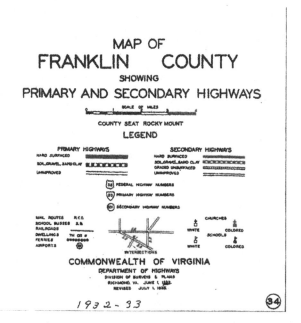

Figure 3.   This section of the 1932-33 Virginia Highway Map shows the roads leading into Ferrum. (Virginia Department of Transportation)

Buchholtz's 1859 map of Virginia shows a road in this area originating at the western base of "Brown's Hill Mt." proceeding northeast toward Cobb's (Cook's) Knob and crossing the Carolina Road at about present day Waidsboro then continuing on to Rocky Mount.

Slone describes an extension of the road leading from Long Branch and Endicott communities by way of Rock Spring Church and entering Ferrum near the Keys residence (P. Slone, Monograph 4). The road then turned northeast, followed Story Creek along the base of Cook's Knob to Waidsboro (today's Old Ferrum Road-Rte. 864). The Keys family resided on the prominent hill on the west side of the railroad tracks overlooking the village. Today's Nolens Hill Road crosses this hill and passes within a few feet of the grave of Elkanah Keys. A long abandoned road bed exists exactly where Slone indicates the road entered the village. Rock Spring Church was about two to three miles west of Ferrum near Rte. 781 and the William Martin farm. The original road came directly over the hill (now part of the Claire Young family property) and down into Ferrum; it

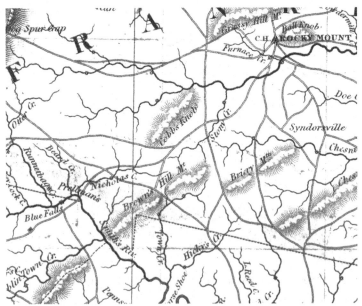

Figure 4.   The Ludwig Von Buchholtz map of 1859 shows what may have been the "Brown Hill Turnpike". (Courtesy of the Franklin County Historical Society)

did not turn south onto Rte. 623 as King Richard Road does today.

The most significant change to the roads in Ferrum came on April 25, 1968, when the Ferrum Bypass and the Sheriff Shively Memorial Bridge opened to traffic. Virginia State Highway 40 traffic was routed to the northeast of the village and over the Norfolk and Western Railroad tracks via the new bridge. For the first time since the 1890's, Rte. 40 traffic did not have to negotiate the railroad crossing in the village. The improvements proved a mixed blessing. Rte. 40 traffic avoided the crossing and the delays of slower speeds in the village, but the village businesses saw fewer customers. The results were predictable: the businesses would have to follow the traffic. Soon after the bypass opened, Rocky Mount attorney Ralph Rhodes and businessman Tillie Anderson bought property along the new road from the Nolen family and constructed a modern brick commercial building. By 1972 the new building housed a hardware store, a grocery store with gas pumps, a Laundromat, and a hair salon. Longtime

Figure 5.   The Sheriff Shively Bridge was opened in 1968 and named for a long serving member of the Franklin County Board of Supervisors who represented the Ferrum area. His given name was Sheriff; he never served as county sheriff. (Courtesy of the Blue Ridge Institute)

109

Ferrum businessman Frank Peters and his family operated the hardware and grocery store for a number of years. Danny Perdue, a successful Rocky Mount entrepreneur, bought the building in1996 and extended his Minute Market franchise to Ferrum. Another successful Rocky Mount businessman, L.D. Arrington, opened a Dairy Queen restaurant in1994 just to the west of the Minute Market complex. Around 2012, a Dollar General store opened near the restaurant. Both of these businesses are located on what was formerly the Alexander (Eck) Ingram property behind the razed railroad station. A few hundred yards to the east of the Minute Market on Rte. 40, Worth Carter opened a branch of the First National Bank of Rocky Mount on August 1, 1997. Since 2006, the bank has been a branch of Carter Bank and Trust with strong ties to the village in the persons of branch manager Charlene Peters Robinson and CB&T corporate president Phyllis Quinn Karavatakis, both Ferrum natives. The latter serves also as the chairwoman of the Ferrum College Board of Trustees.

The condition of most of the roads before the passage of the Byrd

Figure 6. *The Carter Bank and Trust built in 2006 stands on the eastern approach to the village. (Courtesy of the Blue Ridge Institute)*

Figure 7.   The Ferrum Minute Market complex, the Dairy Queen, and the Dollar General all opened along the realigned Route 40 approach to the Shively Bridge. (Courtesy of the Blue Ridge Institute)

Highway Act in 1932 would have been atrocious. Before the opening of the railroad in 1892, western Franklin County was effectively isolated as was virtually all of the Blue Ridge. Heavy rain or snow could make roads impassable for weeks, if not months, during the year. Maintenance of the roads was largely the responsibility of the property owners before the twentieth century and varied considerably depending on the land owners' ability and inclination. Periodically, the state would provide a steam powered crusher to pulverize to gravel the rocks farmers had hauled to the road side. Of course, the farmer had to spread the gravel. Unbelievably, farmers were also tasked with plowing up and drag sledding top soil from their fields to be spread and packed down on the roads (K. Goode). Anecdotes abound describing the state of the roads. Before Rte. 40 was paved west of Rocky Mount in 1936, it was not uncommon for people with business in Ferrum to stop at the Rocky Mount train station to enquire about the state of the road. If the road was impassable, people

Figure 8.   The unpaved street in front of the J.K. Hurt building circa 1925. (Courtesy of the Blue Ridge Institute)

would park their cars and catch the next train to Ferrum.

Between 1916 and 1930, automobile ownership increased nationwide from 37,000 to 387,000 (*A History of Roads in Virginia* 30). The growing numbers of cars effectively forced the state to take over the construction and maintenance of highways. In the late 1930's and early 1940's, the

Figure 9.   Dr. Benjamin Beckham in a Model T negotiates the treacherous roads around Ferrum circa 1920. (Courtesy of the Blue Ridge Institute)

state paved Rte. 40 first between Rocky Mount and Ferrum (1936) and then from Ferrum to Rte. 605 at Crossroads (1942-1944). Paving of the remainder of Rte. 40 to the Patrick county line was not completed until 1949. Most of this work was completed largely with convict labor under the watchful eyes of armed guards. The state built a convict labor camp two miles west of Ferrum to house the prisoners for the duration of the project. While some thought it inhumane to use convict labor on public works projects, Phillip Wilson, the first Virginia Highway Commissioner, observed, "the men in the road camps seem satisfied and many have expressed to me a preference for this work to remaining in jail" (*A History of Virginia Roads* 21). In 1994 through the efforts of B.A. Davis, Jr. and then state senator Virgil H. Goode, Jr., the Virginia Legislature designated State Rte. 40 from the Patrick/Franklin line to Rocky Mount the W. Hank Norton Highway in honor of the successful and long-serving Ferrum College football coach.

Chapter 11

The Railroad Story and Stories of the Railroad

In Roanoke, Virginia, in 1887 John C. Moomaw, H.S. Trout, P.L. Terry, David Houston, and others formed the Roanoke and Southern Railway Company having been granted a charter by the Virginia General Assembly in 1886. After the North Carolina legislature granted a charter in 1887, Francis Fries, R.J. Reynolds, H.W. Hanes and others in that same year in Salem, North Carolina, established the Roanoke and Southern Railway Company of North Carolina. The two companies consolidated and began construction on the rail line that would stretch the 122.53 miles between Roanoke and Winston-Salem.

Using both paid and convict labor, the combined companies began work in Henry County, Virginia, only to abandon their original plan and form two construction divisions under a separate independent construction company. Colonel Francis H. Fries headed this company and supervised the actual construction. Division A was to lay the tracks from Winston-Salem to Martinsville, Virginia. Division B had the more difficult mountainous route from Martinsville to Roanoke. Grade elevations were limited to two per cent which required the right of way to follow valleys and river and creek bottoms. Where hills were encountered trestles had to be built to span them or laborers had to cut through them with picks, shovels, horse or mule drawn graders and scrapers. The Summit Cut was the deepest cut on the line and was located

Figure 1.   A Roanoke and Southern construction crew poses before a bridge abutment between Lanahan and Ferrum circa 1891. (Courtesy of Bethany Worley)

a few hundred yards south of the Ferrum station. The hilly terrain around Ferrum proved to be the most difficult challenge on the line; the last rail was laid at Rocky Mount in December of 1891 finally linking Roanoke and Winston-Salem (Crowder).

Colonel Fries was credited personally for working day and night in all kinds of weather to complete the line. Perhaps the real credit should go to the men who wielded the picks and shovels and who wrestled the crossties and the rails into place for the four years 1887 to 1891. An unattributed source in Volume 7 of *Yesterday and Today* describes the horrendous working conditions under which the men and animals labored with mud up to the knees of the horses and over the axles of the wagons. At the deep cut between present-day Franklin Heights Baptist Church and Rocky Mount Elementary School just north of Rocky Mount, the work was done by convicts. The article entitled "Penitentiary Hill" relates, "that many prisoners died, some from illness, but some from being knocked in the heads by irate guards. They were dumped on the wagons and unloaded with the loads of dirt. This was their grave. Others were buried in unmarked graves (*Yesterday and Today* 72)."

Figure 13.   The Franklin Heights Cut just north of Rocky Mount where convict laborers were reportedly buried in unmarked graves. (Courtesy of the Franklin County Historical Society)

Given that construction was behind schedule, that Rocky Mount was literally the last link, and that over $2,000,000 in 1891 dollars ($50,000,000 in today's dollars) was at stake, perhaps such brutality toward workers did occur. At great cost in both human and monetary terms, the line was finished. The first passenger train pulled into the Ferrum station in January 1892, and passenger trains would continue doing so for almost seventy years.

The fast growing Norfolk and Western Railroad Company secured a lease in March 1892 from the Roanoke and Southern for these hard won tracks. Four years later after both railroads experienced financial difficulties, The Norfolk and Western Railway Company bought the Roanoke and Southern Railway Company (Crowder). The line became officially the Winston-Salem Division of the Norfolk and Western; unofficially, of course, it was the "Punkin' Vine" because of its many twists and turns. The Norfolk and Western merged with the Southern Railway in 1982 and became and remains the Norfolk Southern Corporation.

For those old enough to remember, nothing could compete with the

*Figure 2.   A Roanoke and Southern Stock Certificate dated
1887. (Courtesy of John Speidel)*

glory and drama of a huge steam locomotive huffing and chuffing, spewing clouds of steam, belching smoke and cinders from its stack, clanging its bell or sounding its steam whistle. Grown men and women, not just children, stopped whatever they were doing to watch a steam locomotive pull into or pass through Ferrum or, for that matter, a thousand other villages and towns.

Gladys Edwards Willis writes eloquently about her childhood memories of the excitement generated by the arrival of a train in Ferrum in the 1930's:

But the Ferrum of my childhood days was not your humdrum run-of-the-mill wide spot in the road. It had a purpose for being there and hustled and bustled with the life breathed into it by the Norfolk and Western Railroad line going to Roanoke and Winston-Salem.... You couldn't spend more than thirty minutes at Ferrum before it sprang into action, getting ready for a train to come in. First a clicking sound was heard from near the depot which was the cue for the Station Master (Herbert or John Lemons, both stout little men) to strut about the platform in anticipation of its arrival.... A hush fell over the crowds in

Figure 3.   The first Ferrum Railroad Station that served Ferrum from 1892 to about 1920. (Courtesy of the Blue Ridge Institute)

the street, and time seemed to stand still until a low whistle broke the silence, and simultaneously the lights turned red, the bell clanged and the stop sign fell across the railway crossing. Everyone became a prisoner on whichever side of the track he was on. Wagons and flatbed trucks stood ready by the station and people moved to the edge of the platform with their suitcases. The odor of steam and the billow of black smoke preceded the engine as it chugged around the bend, and suddenly Ferrum was divided in half as the train groaned and sighed to a stop in front of the station. Everything around it went into motion, mailbags

Figure 4.   Roanoke and Southern Locomotive No. 1 brought the first passenger train to Ferrum in January 1892. (Courtesy of the Franklin County Historical Society)

Figure 5.   An early passenger train with a mail car, a combination baggage car, and two passenger coaches. (Courtesy of the Norfolk and Western Historical Society)

Figure 6.   The iconic Class K2 streamlined engines pulled the N&W passenger trains through Ferrum for decades. The Class J 611 never ran on the Punkin Vine. (Courtesy of the Norfolk and Western Historical Society)

Figure 7.   A southbound Norfolk and Western diesel engine approaches Ferrum circa 1980. (Courtesy of the Norfolk and Western Historical Society)

were taken off and put on, passengers stepped off and climbed on, people yelled to be heard over the noise of loading and unloading freight cars. (110-11)

The Norfolk and Western was the last major railroad company to abandon steam in favor of diesel locomotives. The last regularly scheduled steam engine in service made its final run for the Norfolk and Western in May, 1960.

Whether powered by steam or diesel, the railroad played an integral part in the life of the village, and many individuals like Willis retained fond memories of the trains that passed through Ferrum. Some of these memories follow. In August 1985, William P. Swartz wrote in *The Mountain Laurel* about a clever solution to the absence of a dining car between Roanoke and Winston-Salem. The "Punkin' Vine" route was too short to make a dining car practical. For a while though an enterprising hotelier in Martinsville offered a unique noon meal service to travelers. The conductor would take meal orders after the train left Roanoke. On offer were basket lunches of country ham, fried chicken or roast beef served on hotel china. When the train reached Ferrum the conductor would pass the meal orders to the station agent who would telegraph them to the agent in Martinsville who in turn would telephone them to the Broad Street Hotel. When the train reached Martinsville, the baskets would be brought on board and delivered to the passengers. Later, the baskets with the dirty dishes would be transferred to a northbound train to be returned to Martinsville. The Norfolk and Western clearly tried to accommodate its passengers and make train travel as convenient and comfortable as possible, even allowing a third party businessman like the Martinsville hotelier to offer a meal service on one of their trains.

Another example of exceptional service the Norfolk and Western provided Ferrum was the willingness of the company to add extra cars for Ferrum Training School students at the beginning and end of the school year and at all holidays. Given that at its height the passenger rail service in Ferrum saw three daily southbound and three daily northbound passenger trains, residents could easily make day trips to Roanoke or Martinsville for shopping, appointments, or just a day out. Traveling by train was not just convenient, it was deemed safe enough even for unaccompanied young women. Ruby Woods Worley remembered her first train ride as a lone teenager to an eye doctor's appointment in Roanoke. The conductor provided her with directions to the doctor's office and instructions on how to catch the afternoon train back to Ferrum. Irene Hatcher Burnett recalled when her mother allowed her and her sister as children, again unchaperoned, to ride the train to Martinsville for an afternoon visit with family. She could not recall how old she was at the time, but she did recall that in their excitement she and her sister crawled under the train car rather than going around the train to get to the station. Perhaps the times were indeed safer, but clearly children were no less daring and unpredictable!

Patricia Haney Carter remembered riding on an open horse drawn wagon

N&W RY. Norfolk&Western

Schedule n effect Nov. 14th, 1915.
LEAVE ROCKY MOUNT:

NORTHBOUND

10:02 A. M.—Daily for Roanoke and intermediate stations. Connects with Main Line trains North, East, and West, with Pullman Sleepers and Dining cars.

5:19 P. M.—Daily for Roanoke, the North and East. Pullman steel electric lighted sleeper Winston-Salem to Harrisburg, Philadelphia, New York. Dining cars North of Roanoke.

7:47 P. M.—Daily for Roanoke and local stations. Pullman Sleeper.

SOUTH BOUND

7:47 A. M.—Daily Winston-Salem and local stations.

10:02 A. M.—Daily for Martinsville and Winston Salem, Wadesboro, Florence and the South. Pullman Sleeper to Winston-Salem and Jacksonville

6:11 P. M.—Daily for Winston - Salem and intermediate stations.

For additional information call on Agent of N. & W. Ry.

W. B. BEVILL, Pass. Traffic Manager,
Roanoke, Va.

W. C. SAUNDERS, Gen. Passenger Agt.,
Roanoke, Va.

Figure 8.   A 1915 N&W Schedule for Rocky Mount shows that six passenger trains served Ferrum daily. (Courtesy of the Franklin County Historical Society)

with her grandfather Sam Ingram from the Ingramville vicinity to Ferrum to meet the ice train. As late as the 1940's, iceboxes were still in common use, and the railroad ran weekly insulated box cars with cargoes of large blocks of ice to supply country folk with this important commodity. Edward Goode remembered that his grandfather and father bought lime by the boxcar load for their farms. The lime had to be off-loaded onto trucks by hand one shovelful at a time. The railroad placed the boxcars onto sidings, but only allowed the farmers or merchants

Norfolk & Western Ry.

Shenandoah Division

Station-Ferrum, Virginia, Furniture & Fixtures- Account 16

	Number	Cost	Amt.	Yrs. in Service
Water Bucket 3 gal.	1	.26	.26	2
Station Settees 10'	2	12.50	25.00	22
" " 14'	1	17.50	17.50	10
Chairs N&W Std.	4	1.22	4.88	3
Seth Thomas Clock	1	12.50	12.50 15	22
Coal Hod	1	.35	.35	1
Desk Poplar 2 drawers	1	27.82	27.82	20
Dipper	1	.10	.10	1
Flags - Red	1	.18	.18	1
" Green & White	1	.08	.08	1
Hatchet	1	.35	.35	2
Lantern - White	1	.65	.65	1
Lamps Bracket	3	.65	1.95	2
Mail Cart	1	12.00	12.00	1
Oil Cans 3 gal.	1	.30 2.25	.30 1.25	4
" " 5 gal.	1	.38	.38	4
Lamp - Post	1	4.50	4.50	5
Platform Scales	1	5.00	5.00 7.00	5
Stationery Case	1	4.75	4.75	10
Water Bbls. Wooden	2	1.00	2.00	2
Fire Buckets	2	.38	.76	5
Stoves Burnside No.1	2	3.86	7.72	5
Stove Pipe Joints	8	.08	.64	3
Brooms New	2	.25	.50	1
Warehouse Trucks	2	5.65	11.30	15
Brackets -Lamp	2	.23	.46	1
Flag - Green	1	.08	.08	1
Lanterns - Green	1	.73	.73	1
" Red	1	.82	.82	1
Gang Board - Steel	1	6.00	6.00	5
Lamp - Desk	1	1.50 75	1.50 75	2
Skids - Wooden 20 ft.	1	19.50	19.50	5
Gang Board - Iron	1	5.00	6.00	10
Safe - Iron	1	5.00	5.00	15
Filing Case 12x22	1	4.76 9	4.76 9	8

$28484

Figure 9.   The Ferrum Station Inventory for 1916 was quite detailed and included coal hods, water bucket dippers, and stove pipe joints. (Courtesy of the Norfolk and Western Historical Society)

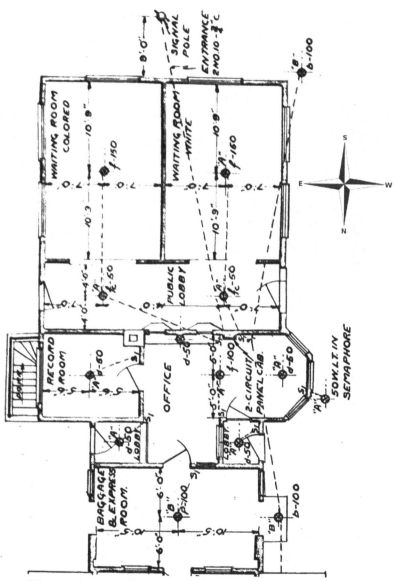

Figure 10.   *The Ferrum Station layout from 1926 shows the
separate ticket window and waiting room for Blacks. Attached to the
north side of the station was a 100' x 20' freight room (not pictured)
with a 10' open platform on three sides. (Courtesy of the Norfolk and
Western Historical Society)*

Figure 11.   The fine old Ferrum station was razed in 1970.
(Courtesy of the Franklin County Historical Society)

forty-eight hours to off load the contents lest "overage" charges began to accumulate.

Paul Simms, the owner of a small country store in the Hurd's Branch community west of Ferrum, found it cost effective in the early 1900's to buy large quantities of goods and have them shipped by rail to Ferrum a few times a year. To avoid the overage costs, he built a small warehouse or packing house across the road from the railroad station to store his goods until he needed them at his business (Merchant, p.142).

In the autumn during the depression years, Ruby Woods Worley recalled that the railroad ran what she described as the Booster Train. Presumably businesses and civic groups donated children's school supplies and passed out pencils, erasers, rulers, tablets, etc. to children waiting by the tracks. Evidently, local Ferrum merchants extended the booster idea to other communities because Gladys Edwards Willis in her book *Goin' Up Shootin' Creek* mentions receiving school supplies as well as balloons and ice cream treats from men in funny hats driving decorated automobiles (46).

Colonel James Stanley recalled the amazingly efficient and rapid catalog mail order service offered by the competing companies of Sears and Roebuck and Montgomery Ward. If a mail order went out on the first northbound train of the day, the Montgomery Ward distribution center in Baltimore could have the order to the customer in three days! With a distribution center in Atlanta, the Sears and Roebuck order took four days. Even in the 1930's and 1940's, Stanley said folks preferred the faster service of Montgomery Ward.

During the years of peak service, six passenger/mail trains, three going north and three going south, stopped in Ferrum daily. A 1915 Norfolk and Western Time Table for Rocky Mount shows northbound trains leaving at 10:02 AM, 5:19 PM, and 7:47 PM while southbound trains left at 7:47 AM, 10:02 AM, and 6:11 PM. (To calculate the departure times for trains leaving Ferrum, subtract thirteen minutes from the Rocky Mount departure time for northbound trains and add thirteen minutes to the Rocky Mount departure time for southbound trains.) As the roads gradually improved after the *1932 Virginia Highway Act* making automobile travel easier, passenger train service was reduced. By 1938, there were only four passenger trains per day. In February 1961, when daily passenger train service to Ferrum ended after sixty-nine years, the Norfolk and Western was running one southbound passenger train that came through the village at about 1:00 PM and one northbound train that passed through at about 5:00 PM.

Well before the discontinuance of passenger service in 1961, the railroad had eliminated the station agent, and passengers were on their own to raise a flag to signal the train to stop to take on passengers. After both passenger and freight service to Ferrum ended in the 1960's, the fine old station was used as a warehouse for a while and then was unceremoniously razed in August of 1970. The Norfolk Southern Corporation still owns the land on which the station stood.

From the 1890's to the 1950's, the station agent was an integral part of village life. The station agent who relayed the meal orders by telegraph to Martinsville had to be a jack of many, if not all, trades. In addition to managing the station and overseeing considerable incoming as well as outgoing mail and freight, he had to sell passenger tickets. Because of racial segregation policies, he would have had to maintain and supervise separate ticket windows, waiting rooms and accommodations for white and Black passengers. (On board the trains, the seating would be strictly separate, sometimes in separate rail cars.)

In addition to managing all the paperwork, the agent would have to be a competent telegrapher. Before radios on trains and telephones in stations, the telegraph was the means of communication directly between stations and indirectly with the trains themselves. Once received by telegraph and written down, paper messages would be clipped onto long-handled wooden hoops and held out to the passing train by the agent. The conductor on the train would simply hold out his arm and catch the hoop with the attached message or order.

Colonel James Stanley recalled how fascinated he was by the ability of Ferrum station agent John Lemons to transcribe Morse code messages into words instantly by ear without having to write down the dots and dashes. The Lemons family whose large, handsome house stood on the hill overlooking the village, had several members who worked as agents or employees of the Norfolk and Western including A.L. Lemons, Herbert Lemons, John Lemons, Willard (Bill) Lemons and Myrtle Lemons Quinn. And though never an employee, even Bessie Mae Lemons learned Morse code perhaps to help her younger brothers hone their skills.

Telegraphers were phased out by the railroad in the 1930's only to find themselves in serious demand by the U.S. armed services in World War II when coders, code readers and code breakers were critically needed.

The railroad crossing at Ferrum did not have warning lights until electricity and electric relays were available on the railroad in 1926. Crossing gates did not appear until the 1950's. Despite there being two hundred yards of visibility up and down the tracks, and despite trains always sounding loud whistles and ringing bells at all road crossings, at least a few men managed to get themselves killed at or near the Ferrum crossing. The *Bedford Bulletin Democrat* newspaper of November 30, 1899, reported that Ferrum resident Alonzo Crum was killed on the railroad (L. Stanley, 2016 11). James Hollandsworth in his notes about attending Brown Hill School around 1900 stated that John Smith, the father of one of his school mates, was killed along with his team of mules by a train while trying to cross the tracks just south of Ferrum near the

Figure 12.   A view of Ferrum looking southeastward showing several freight cars waiting to be loaded circa 1915. (Courtesy of the Blue Ridge Institute)

Foster Stave Mill.

Though tragic, another fatal accident took on a comic dimension. A certain alcoholic with distinctive red hair and known locally as "Red" habitually walked the tracks near the village. One day when the badly mauled body of a red-haired man was found along the tracks, everyone assumed it was poor "Red." When "Red" himself showed up among the onlookers and was told by someone that all gathered had thought that the deceased fellow was him. "Red" is reported to have said dismissively, "Well, hell—I took one look at him and knowed it twarn't me!"

Another humorous liquor related anecdote involves the "Punkin' Vine" branch of the Norfolk and Western and deals with a sleepy conductor on a southbound passenger train. After this certain conductor had checked all the tickets of passengers who boarded in Roanoke, he sat down to rest his feet for a few minutes. A mistake in as much as the rocking of the train lulled him sound asleep. As fate would have it, a passenger had come on board with a quart jar of Franklin County's finest which he had been liberally sampling. For reasons known only to him, the now thoroughly intoxicated man with jar in hand decided to walk down the aisle of the car. Just as he reached the seat of the sleeping conductor, he accidentally dropped the glass jar which shattered on the floor with a loud crash and sent the pungent fumes of moonshine through the car. Startled out of a sound sleep by the breaking glass and smelling the unmistakable odor of the whiskey, instinct and training kicked in simultaneously. The conductor leaped to his feet and in his best and clearest baritone called out, "Ferrum, Ferrum. Next stop Ferrum."

Alcohol was not thought to have been involved in the only known collision of passenger trains on the "Punkin' Vine" which occurred in Rocky Mount in March, 1944. Inexplicably, both a northbound train and a southbound train were diverted onto the same siding. The resulting low speed crash damaged both engines and injured several passengers, some severely enough to require hospitalization in Roanoke (*Rocky Mount, Virginia Railroadin' Since 1880*).

Both Marshall Wingfield and Pedro Slone emphasize the importance of the coming of the Roanoke and Southern Railroad in 1892 to the founding and the flourishing of the village. As noted, following bankruptcy and reorganization the Roanoke and Southern became the Norfolk and Western Railroad in 1896. With the railroad came the opportunity for both passenger and freight service into what had been a remote and difficult to access area of Franklin County. Until the advent of paved roads in the 1930's and 1940's, the train provided travelers the safest and fastest mode of transportation. The writer's own grandfather, Luther A. Smith as a young man took advantage of the railroad to make his way to Texas and sample for himself what was left of frontier life. He stayed but a short while before a self-confessed homesickness led him back home over the same rails he had ridden just a few months before. The availability of a train depot within a half mile of the proposed site of what would become the Ferrum Training School played a critical part in the Methodist Church's decision to locate the school in Ferrum in 1913. Frank Hurt in his *A History of Ferrum College* provides a charming description of the school's first principal, Dr. Benjamin Beckham and his family arriving in Ferrum by train, taking their supper at the boarding house of Berta Nolen Boothe (Mrs. John O. Boothe), and then walking to their home on what would become the campus of the school (27). Hundreds upon hundreds of Ferrum students would follow in the Beckhams' footsteps over the coming years until 1961 when all passenger service ended.

Hurt also notes that Ferrum after 1892 became "one of the largest shipping points on this railway for logs, lumber, crossties, chestnuts, barrel-staves, tan-bark, canned goods, and manufactured oak and locust insulator pins"(Hurt, *History* 23). Photographs dating from about 1913 clearly show large piles of crossties and posts as well as wagon loads of lumber waiting to be loaded on to rail cars on the siding across from J.K. Hurt and Company (Webb 23)(*see ch. 3, fig. 10*).

Chapter 12

Factories and Assorted Other Businesses

A cannery or a canning factory in the early twentieth century was usually no more than a covered shed or an open outbuilding as the work was strictly seasonal lasting from mid-summer to early autumn. Cannery owners would buy blackberries, beans, peaches, tomatoes, and apples from local farmers and residents. The going rate for many years for berries was 25 cents per gallon and 25 cents for a bushel (60 lbs.) of tomatoes. Near the end of the era of local commercial canning in the mid-1940's, tomatoes sold for the princely sum of 80 cents per bushel. Factory workers, usually women, would first inspect the produce for insects, stems, green or rot. Workers would peal peaches, apples and tomatoes and would string and break (snap) beans on a piece work basis meaning they were paid not by the hour but by the quantity they produced. They would then pack the fruit or vegetables into tin cans and solder on a lid with an open steam hole or vent. After the cans were processed in large vats of boiling water, the steam holes were sealed with solder, and the cans were labeled and put in cases for shipment by rail. Most of the cans came from the Continental Can Company in Roanoke, and the labels were printed in Bedford by the Piedmont Label Company (Hudson 92).

Early in the twentieth century George Menefee and J. K. Hurt operated the Hurt Canning Company presumably somewhere in the complex of buildings Hurt owned on the west side of the railroad tracks.

The Ferrum Supply Company owned in 1915 by D. A. Nicholson, T. C. Nicholson and J. H. Nicholson operated a cannery on the east side of the rail road tracks near the Norfolk and Western station close to the original site of the Supply Company main store building. D. A. Nicholson and A. L. Lemons operated a Wholesale Grocery and Feed business as well as a cannery on the west side of the rail road tracks directly opposite the train station. Creed King Lemons also owned a tomato canning factory just south of Ferrum near Prillaman Switch (Rte. 767) (*Callaway of Yesterday* 56).

The canneries in Ferrum and nearby canneries in Nola, Waidsboro and Endicott shipped thousands of cases of canned goods during the heyday of local canneries. According to the *Virginia Business Directory*, thirty-one canneries were operating in Franklin County in 1917 (Salmon 351). This is probably an under count, however, because in a *Roanoke Times* article dated May 25, 1913, describing a meeting of the Roanoke Canners Association, Mr. W.E. Flora of Wirtz is quoted as saying that Franklin County had ten large canneries and about 100 small ones and that the 1912 product was over 125,000 cases of tomatoes alone.

Perhaps not surprisingly, some canning operations were not altogether

Figure 1.   A typical cannery often consisted of little more than a covered shed. (Courtesy of the Franklin County Historical Society)

successful. Becky Merchant relates in her book *Over in the Country* that her grandfather Paul Simms raised and canned "government" tomatoes during World War I. Despite his good intentions to aid in the war effort, the government refused to buy his canned tomatoes when it was discovered he had failed to weigh the contents of each can and could not certify that each can contained the required one pound of tomatoes. Unwilling to lose money, not to mention waste perfectly good food, Simms put the canned tomatoes on the shelves of his store and sold the lot. He did not can any more tomatoes, however (Merchant 138).

For many years Ferrum Training School as a part of its work study program operated a cannery to process locally grown fruits and vegetables in the summer for use in the school cafeteria throughout the school year (Merchant 197).

From about 1900 to 1920, the milling and manufacture of wooden barrel staves was big business in Franklin County. Wooden barrels were used to contain all types of goods including flour, apples, potatoes, whiskey, cider, and vinegar. At least three stave mills and factories operated near Ferrum. *The Franklin County Partnership Book #1* shows that G. A. Menefee, H.E. Menefee, H. N. Menefee, G.C. Payne and V.H. Payne founded the Ferrum Stave Manufacturing Company on December 22, 1897. The purpose of the company was "to buy, manufacture, and sell

Figure 2.   Molasses being canned on the Ferrum Training School campus. (Courtesy of the Blue Ridge Institute)

137

*Figure 3.   A selection of labels from products canned in the
Ferrum area in the early twentieth century. (Courtesy of the Blue
Ridge Institute)*

ROANOKE VALLEY CANNING CO.

GROWERS CONTRACT

****

THIS CONTRACT made and entered into this the _27_ day of _April_ by and between _Ingram_ party of first part hereinafter called the grower, and ROANOKE VALLEY CANNING CO., party of the second part hereinafter called the packers.

WITNESSETH: That the grower agrees and binds himself to plant, cultivate and grow _2½_ acres of land in tomatoes during the season of _1945_ the same to be transplanted as early in the season as weather will permit with plants grown from seed bought from said packers. The said grower agrees to use the proper grade and amount of fertilizer for the growth and development of the tomatoes grown on said acreage; further that he will thoroughly cultivate the said acreage by keeping the land free from weeds and grass so that the tomatoes will properly mature and to deliver all tomatoes produced upon said acreage that will GRADE SOUND RED RIPE stock down to 2 inches in diameter (small tomatoes to be smooth) to packers' canning factory located

Endicott between the hours of 7 A. M. and 5 P. M. of each working day of the week, except Saturdays. No tomatoes are to be delivered on Saturdays without permission from said packers. Tomatoes that are green on one side, not fully developed in size or color, or bruised, jammed or over-ripe will not be considered merchandise, any load container, hamper or basket containing more than 15 per cent of tomatoes which are not merchantable will be subject to dock or refused.

It is agreed that all the tomatoes above described and grown under this contract are the bought property of the packers and shall not be resold or delivered to any other party or place. No green tomatoes are to be sold off this acreage.

Packers agree to pay the said grower _0.81_ per bushel of 60 pounds net weight for all sound red ripe tomatoes suitable for canning purposes produced upon the above specified acreage that are delivered to their factory and accepted.

Said tomatoes are to be delivered in standard crates or baskets to be furnished by the said packers and are to be returned to the factory at the end of the season.

It is agreed by both parties to this contract that all tomatoes delivered and accepted during the packing season of _1945_ shall be paid for on or before November 30, _1945_.

In case of destruction of packers' factory by fire or by the elements or if for any unavoidable cause the packers are unable to receive tomatoes grown, the packers shall have the right to limit the delivery of the tomatoes grown on said acreage.

The grower acknowledges receipt of $1.00 cash in hand to bind this contract.

Witness the following signatures this the _27_ of _April_, _1945_.

_____ Grower.   **ROANOKE VALLEY CANNING CO.,**

SIGNED IN DUPLICATE   By _H. M. Shively_

A war time Growers Contract for an Endicott canning factory from 1945 agrees to pay the farmer eighty-one cents for a bushel of sound tomatoes. (Courtesy of Peggy Ingram Edwards)

139

lumber, staves, barrels, and sassafras oil." According to John Salmon this enterprise produced and shipped thirty-five railroad cars of staves in 1899 (340). A Norfolk and Western 1898 Engineering and Maintenance of Way drawing shows the location of a proposed packing (warehouse) for the stave company on a site at the intersection Rte. 40 and Rte. 767 where the Ferrum Mercantile building would be built later. The most likely location of the mill itself would be on land adjoining that site on the east side of the railroad tracks. This property was within a few yards of the railroad tracks, greatly facilitating shipping. Like so many Ferrum businesses and houses, this stave company was destroyed by fire.

Frank Mills in an article in *Callaway of Yesterday* describes the mill owned by Ferrum businessmen Creed Lemons, D. A. (Dave) Nicholson, and H. N. Prillaman (56). This factory received dried rough cut oak and poplar staves from stave mills that used tube bladed saws to create the characteristic bend in the stave; then the factory workers shaped, dressed and grooved the staves before bundling them for shipment by rail to cooperages where they would be formed in to barrels (*Callaway of Yesterday* 56). James Hollandsworth in an article for the *Henry County Journal* in 1968 describes working as a young man in another Ferrum stave factory, the Foster Barrel Stave Company founded around 1900 by James Robert Foster (1881- 1934). Hollandsworth not only details the stave making process, but he also describes the economic impact the factory had on the community for the twenty years it operated. After 1920, demand for barrels dropped with the introduction of cloth bags, glass and paper containers. Apple shippers continued to use barrels until the 1940's when they were replaced by wooden crates and later by cardboard boxes.

According to Hollandsworth, the stave factory workers did not receive their wages in cash but rather in company script which could only be spent in the company store. The lumbermen who brought logs to the mill also had to take payment in script. Yet Hollandsworth is clearly grateful to the factory for, as he put it, "The establishment of the barrel stave mill meant employment for 18 men and boys when it was in operation." He, even after fifty years, remembered and listed the names of these "men and boys" he worked with: Martin Brim, Jim Haymaker, Sam Turner, Joe Moore, Sandy Craig, Henry Carter, Charlie Carter,

Figure 4.   J.K. Hurt and A.F. Ingram opened the insulator pin and bracket mill in Ferrum 1913. (Courtesy of the Blue Ridge Institute)

William "Buck" Hollandsworth, Butler Ferguson, Jim Kidd, Dan Tensley, Joe Frith, Louis Frith, Emmitt Massey, Lawrence Smith, John Barber, Jim Greer, Alec White, and Walter Edwards. He mentions the men who ran the company store: Jim Haymaker, John Goode, Hamp Ramsey, and Nick Prillaman. He goes on to name thirty-eight farmers who lived near and benefited from the mill.

The practice of payment in company store script persisted well into the 1950's. The last commodity to be shipped from Ferrum by rail was cord wood in stacks measuring 4x4x8 feet. Destined for paper pulp mills, the wood arrived by truck and was off-loaded by hand onto waiting rail cars. Ferrum Mercantile would only buy the wood for a combination of cash and store script (Gearhart).

Another industry in Ferrum was the insulator pin and bracket mill founded in 1913 by J. K. Hurt and operated by his son-in-law Alexander F. (Eck) Ingram (1886-1975). The factory made brackets and wooden pins for the glass insulators to which electric wires were attached on telegraph and telephone poles. According to an unsourced newspaper clipping from 1934 in the Franklin County Historical Society collection, huge quantities of the pins made in Ferrum were used by both the U.S. Government and allied powers during the World War 1914-1918. This factory sat a few hundred yards west of the railroad crossing well behind the Hurt complex of buildings. Ironically, the factory was spared in the March 1940 fire that effectively destroyed Hurt and Company only to be burned to the ground four months later in July 1940. Ingram rebuilt the mill and continued to operate it until the 1950's (P. Slone, Monograph 14).

About 1897, Isaac W. (Ike) Ferguson (1865-1959) began a grist mill and a saw mill in the Story Creek bottom a few hundred yards west of the railroad station. The site today is directly opposite the Ferrum College Police Station on Rte.40. Ferguson ran the grist mill and ground corn for local farmers until the 1950's (P. Slone, Monograph 13). There are references to another grist mill in the village operated by J. K. Hurt, and it may have been located to the north of the Ferguson mill on Story Creek.

Across the road from the Ferguson grist mill, I. W. Ferguson's brother Rufus Ferguson (1880-1956) operated a blacksmith's shop. As long as folks had to rely on horses and horse drawn vehicles and equipment,

Figure 5.   Elegant Woodworks operates on the site of the 1937 Ferrum Veneer Corporation. (Courtesy of the Blue Ridge Institute)

blacksmiths were in constant demand. They also fashioned a variety of tools and implements including shovels, hoes, mattocks, plows, harrow teeth, hooks, and firedogs. According to the *Virginia Business Directory* between 1906 and 1917, a span of just eleven years, however, the number of blacksmiths in Franklin County dropped from forty to twenty-one reflecting the impact of early automobiles (Salmon 338). In 1917 county residents could buy a Ford T-Model for as little as $390 (Salmon 338). Other blacksmiths that operated shops in Ferrum around 1900 included John W. Dowdy (1858-1917), Luther Holdren, James Collins, Neil Janney (1875-1943), and Wiley Underwood (P. Slone, Monograph 14). The *Business Directory* showed that Ferrum had one livery stable in 1906 which provided riders and teamsters fodder and shelter for their animals and presumably provided a hack (horse-drawn cab) service to rail passengers arriving at the Ferrum station and in need of transportation to their destination. A similar hack service was advertised by the Rocky Mount Livery Company in 1908 (Salmon 339).

In 1937 in the midst of the Great Depression, Ferrum Veneer Corporation began operations offering sorely needed employment to about fifty people. The factory sliced thin sheets of wood veneer from huge logs delivered to the site by truck. The sheets of veneer were then shipped to the furniture manufacturers in Henry County. The Franklin County Clerk of the Courts *Partnership Book #1* lists the original Board of Directors as Thomas B. Stanley (President of Stanley Furniture and later Governor of Virginia), R.E. Weaver, J. A. Chapman, J. V. Webb, C. L. Ross, G.W. Nolen, and T.A. Stanley. J. V. Webb and Howard King were the first plant managers succeeded by Robert Armstrong and G.L. Martin, Jr. The plant's steam whistle that was audible for about a mile woke the village at 6 A.M. every weekday morning for decades. When the Ferrum Volunteer Fire Department was organized in 1958, the shrill veneer plant whistle in repeated short blasts served as the fire alarm to summon the volunteers.

The veneer operation ceased in the 1960's and was replaced by a molded plastics manufacturer that made decorative plastic components for use in the Stanley furniture factories in Bassett and Martinsville. A cabinet making business, Elegant Woodworking, now occupies the site.

Figure 6.   The "Silk Mill" water tower still stands. (Courtesy of the Blue Ridge Institute)

On a hill almost directly opposite the site of the veneer plant on the east side of the railroad tracks, Virginia Mills Corporation built a modern brick factory that was always referred to locally as the "silk mill." Beginning operation in 1948, the mill spun and wove natural and synthetic fibers, yarns and threads for fabrics for many years. The Board of Directors listed in the *Partnership Book #1* included J.D. Pell, C. C. Lee, T. L. Peak, W.N. Angle, R. N. Robertson, G. W. Nolen, and G. Claire Young. The J. P. Stevens Company acquired and operated the mill in the 1960's. After the mill closed as a part of the general collapse of the U.S. textile industry, Leo Scott relocated his expanding

Figure 7.   The 1948 Virginia Mills Corporation "Silk Mill" as it appeared in 2019. (Courtesy of the Blue Ridge Institute)

cabinet manufacturing operations to the silk mill site.

Scott began his cabinet making business modestly enough in his basement in the 1950's. Ambitious and hardworking, he built his business into one of the most successful enterprises in the region and spawned several other independent cabinet manufacturing businesses in the area. He also founded KC Farms, a cattle breeding and raising business. Today, Aqua O2 Waste Water Treatment Systems, Inc., formerly Aquarobic International, occupies most of the old silk mill building.

Although the iconic sound of the steam whistle of the Ferrum Veneer plant is long gone, the imposing ten-story silk mill water tank still towers over the village and serves as a reminder of a time when manufacturing was an important part of the life of the village.

Other factories that operated for a comparatively short period in Ferrum: Virginia Apparel Company set up a sewing operation in the old Ferrum Mercantile building; Bassett-Walker manufactured fleece wear in a modern shell building on what was formerly the Pinckard property about a mile west of the village on Rte. 40. Today, this building is owned by James Shively and houses the Gaubatz Painting Company.

Another short-lived business located in the Ferrum Mercantile building was a modern supermarket operated by Jack Menefee, son of

Figure 8.   The Ferrum Mercantile Building from the 1920's is home to Kat's Hidden Treasures in 2019. (Courtesy of the Blue Ridge Institute)

George Menefee one of the first merchants in the village in the 1890's. Ferrum Supermarket opened in the early 1960's and offered a greater range of fresh fruit and vegetables as well as frozen foods than was generally available in other local grocery stores. The Supermarket also had a trained fulltime butcher, Harvey Thompson, who cut fresh meat to order. Though profitable, the business did not produce the revenue Menefee was accustomed to in his other highly successful pin ball and juke box business. He closed the market after only three or four years. During the 1980's, Leo Scott used the space as a part of his cabinet making operation. Hidden Treasures, an antique/thrift shop business owned by Stephanie Boyle and Katrina Harrison, uses the old Mercantile building today.

In the early 1950's, Ferrum Mercantile began selling farm machinery and built a large open front cinder block building to assemble and display the machines. The building was two hundred yards south of the main Mercantile building on the corner of Woodcott Road and Rte.767. Leo Scott converted this building to residential apartments in the 1960's. Through the decades that followed, Scott built several apartment

Figure 9. *These apartments were built by Leo Scott in the 1960's on the site of a farm machinery buisness operated by Ferrum Mercantile. (Courtesy of the Blue Ridge Institute)*

*Figure 10.   The Mead Hollandsworth/Claire Young house built
in 1917 sits on the hill directly opposite the Ferrum railroad crossing.
(Courtesy of the Blue Ridge Institute)*

buildings in and around the village. Today, Ferrum College owns most of
these buildings and uses them for student housing.

A number of garages and filling stations have served the village over
the years since the automobile first arrived on the scene in the years

*Figure 11.   This service station was built by Mike Minucci in the
1950's. (Courtesy of the Blue Ridge Institute)*

Figure 12.   Ferrum Muffler and Auto Shop operates on the site of the original J.K. Hurt Garage and later Young's Garage. (Courtesy of the Blue Ridge Institute)

between 1910 and 1920. Predictably enough, J. K. Hurt built the first garage just north of the Ferrum Bank close to his other businesses on the main street of the village. In 1928 he sold the garage to Claire Young who ran the garage and adjoining filling station until 1974. Over the years, Young expanded and modernized the garage. For a short while, he sold Whippet automobiles, but apparently the vehicles were too low to the ground to be practical on the rough roads of the area (Willis 118). On the east side of the railroad tracks G.L. Martin, Herman Shively, Guy W. Nolen and C. Buford Nolen established Ferrum Garage and a Chevrolet dealership. In 1959, Herman Shively sold his share of the business to Guy Nolen who operated the dealership for a short while before selling the franchise to Winfred E. Stanley. Stanley relocated to Stuart in the 1960's.

Marvin Brammer built a successful garage business just down the street from Young's Garage on the west side of the tracks. Herbert Bowles, who was a trained and certified General Motors mechanic for Ferrum Garage, opened his own garage around 1959 when Herman Shively bought a Chevrolet Dealership in Alta Vista and left Ferrum. He located his garage on the west side of the tracks near the intersection of Rte. 623 and Timberline Road on former Menefee property. Bowles' wife was the former Myrtle Menefee daughter of H. E. Menefee , an early Ferrum merchant and property owner. In the late 1950's, Mike Minucci built a service station about three hundred yards east of the railroad crossing on then Rte. 40. Hugh Peters, Phillip Martin, Eddie Hale, Glen Cannaday, and James (Popeye) Shively and others have operated this business down through the years.

Today the only surviving garage in the village, the Ferrum Muffler and Auto Shop, is owned and operated by Ricky Green, fittingly enough the grandson of Claire Young who ran a garage on this site from 1928 to 1974.

Chapter 13

The Risky Whiskey Business

The great federal conspiracy trial of 1935 shined a spotlight on the symbiotic relationship between the Norfolk and Western Railroad and the economics of Ferrum and all of western Franklin County. Several books have been written about the illicit liquor business in Franklin County and the great reckoning that came in 1935 when the federal government cracked down on the bootleggers and their suppliers. But no history of Ferrum, no matter how slight, can overlook the economic impact on the village of the illegal moonshine business between 1916 and 1935.

In the 1920's, an incredibly lucrative but illegal business opportunity would present itself to the merchants of Ferrum. From the time the early settlers first brought their distilling skills from Scotland and Ireland, both legal and illegal whiskey making had thrived in western Franklin County. Before the 1916 Mapp Act which established statewide prohibition in Virginia and the 1918 Volstead Act that prohibited the manufacture, sale, or distribution of liquor in the United States, the residents of western Franklin County had been able to make whiskey with only minimal interference from the government. Mountain folk considered whiskey making a birthright handed down to them by their Scots-Irish ancestors, and more importantly they depended on it as one of their very few

Figure 1.   Pictured here are a group of still hands at a turnip-style still around 1916. (Courtesy of the Blue Ridge Institute)

sources of ready money. As early as the 1780's, the citizens of Henry and Patrick counties petitioned the Virginia General Assembly to protest the imposing of a tax of nine cents per gallon on all distilled spirits. They argued that this tax would deprive them "…of one of the blessings God and nature have given us because we have not the money to pay the excise" (Greer, *Genesis* 103).

Before prohibition, legal stills, large and small, dotted all of Franklin County. In 1893 -1894, the *Business Directory* listed seventy-seven licensed, tax-paying distilleries, but by 1917 there were none (Salmon 396); no reckoning of illegal moonshine stills is possible. Pedro Slone reports that T.F. Bailey a licensed distiller in North Carolina moved all of his distilling equipment to a site just northeast of Ferrum (on Route 864) when that state voted for prohibition. His decision to remove to Ferrum was hardly a random one given that Franklin County repeatedly defeated any attempt to vote the county dry. He famously shipped his Virginia licensed whiskey back to his North Carolina customers by railroad express until Virginia and national prohibition shut him down permanently (P. Slone, Monograph 7).

Ironically, but not surprisingly, prohibition took Franklin County moonshining from small business status to an almost industrial scale in the 1920's and 1930's earning the county the moniker 'Moonshine Capital' of the country. The 1931 Wickersham Report commissioned by President Herbert Hoover described Franklin County as "one of the

Figure 2.   This whiskey bottle shows the logo of Ferrum licensed distiller T.F. Bailey. (Courtesy of the Franklin County Historical Society)

wettest spots in the United States" (Greer, *Conspiracy* 20).

In the liquor conspiracy trial of 1935, a Norfolk and Western chief auditor testified that between January 1928 and March 1935, Ferrum Mercantile Company had taken delivery of 65,370 lbs. of meal, 196,050 lbs. of malt, 1,239,303 lbs. of feed, and 12,863,425 lbs. of sugar. Another 6,516,208 lbs. of sugar was delivered to Ferrum by rail presumably to other merchants in the village (Greer, *Conspiracy* 202). Another Norfolk and Western record of shipments to Ferrum in a comparable period shows 115,000 lbs. of copper, 1,250,000 five-gallon tin cans, 7,320 kegs and barrels and 35 tons of yeast (Greer, *Conspiracy* 622). Assuming all the five-gallon tin cans were filled with moonshine and sold, then 6,250,000 gallons of illegal whiskey made its way out of the Ferrum area between

Figure 3.   Some of the 1.25 million 5-gallon tin cans shipped by rail to Ferrum are pictured here. (Courtesy of the Blue Ridge Institute)

1928 and 1935. If as Greer reports the bootlegger could charge somewhere between a low of 70 cents to a high of $2.25 per gallon, the average would be about $1.50 per gallon (Greer, *Conspiracy* 164, 165,185,207). The Ferrum bootleggers would then have grossed about $10,000,000 in the 1930's (Conservatively $120,000,000 in current dollars). With a street value of $6 per gallon (Greer, *Conspiracy* 302) retailers would have netted some $37,500,000 (Again, conservatively $450,000,000 in current dollars).

Suffice it to say moonshine was very big business in Ferrum, and the Wickersham Commission conclusion that in Franklin County "99 people out of 100 are making, or have some connection with, illicit liquor" might have been only a slight exaggeration when applied to the good citizens of Ferrum (Greer, *Conspiracy* 20). As is always the case, however, a few profited exorbitantly while the average still hand barely put food on the table. One, C. Taft Menefee, testified in the 1935 conspiracy trial that he was paid $1.50 a day (Greer, *Conspiracy* 157). C.B. Collins, another still worker, testified he was paid five cents per gallon produced at the end of a run (Greer, *Conspiracy* 173). For a 500-gallon run produced in a three to four week period, Collins would have earned about one dollar per day.

Figure 4.   This picture clearly shows the primitive and difficult working conditions at a still site around 1930. (Courtesy of the Blue Ridge Institute)

Chapter 14

Law and Order

Before the 1930's, the people of Ferrum traditionally depended on the Franklin County Sheriff and his deputies to provide law and order in and around the village. Late in 1931, however, some of the residents of Ferrum petitioned the Circuit Court Judge Peter Hairston Dillard to appoint an independent county policeman to protect the people of the village. The text of the petition which was written on the Bank of Ferrum stationery read:

> We, the undersigned, respectfully request the appointment of V.T. Foster as a County Policeman for Franklin County, Virginia. Mr. Foster was a Deputy Sheriff and performed the duties of the office faithfully and honestly and was a great factor in preserving peace and order in and around Ferrum, Virginia. We feel his appointment would provide protection to the law-abiding citizens of the community.

The petition was signed by B.M. Beckham, Mrs. B.M. Beckham, B.M. Beckham, Jr., J.K. Hurt, J.M. Green, C.L. Ross, C.A. Hickman, M.S. Hollandsworth, J.A. Moore, Bill Barrow, C. Hurt, R.L. Cassell, J.H. Hunt, D.E. Bryant, I.C. Brammer, G.I. Beckner, G.A. Turner, S.J. Mullins, B.M. Bowling, V.A. Dodson, Oliver Young, J.E. Ferguson, Bessie Lemons, W.H. King, A.F. Ingram, Mrs. A.F. Ingram, Frank Hurt,

R.E. Whitehead, Mrs. R.E. Whitehead, O.W. Lemons, and F.F. Turner.

The petition which was dated December 31, 1931, was followed by a letter dated January 1, 1932, to Judge Dillard. "It is with pleasure the citizens of Ferrum have petitioned your honor for the appointment of county officer Mr. V.T. Foster who has served as deputy sheriff and whose services have been most satisfactory and whose conduct has been most excellent." This letter on Ferrum Drug Company stationery was signed by J.K. Hurt, C.W. Hurt, J.M. Green, G.O. Buckner R.P., W.H. King, and B.M. Beckham, Jr. (Copies of both the petition and the letter are on display in the Franklin County History Museum). Obviously, most of the prominent businessmen and professionals saw a need for a full-time peace officer for the village. Interestingly, the petition specifically requested protection for the law-abiding citizens, clearly implying that some of the citizens were not law-abiding.

It should be noted that none of the petitioners were involved in the liquor conspiracy trial of 1935. Further, it should be noted that none of the prominent Ferrum businessmen who were indicted in the 1935

Figure 1. The Lewis Bridges house still stands some two hundred yards east of the Ferrum railroad crossing. (Courtesy of the Blue Ridge Institute)

criminal proceedings had signed the 1932 petition.

As the liquor conspiracy trial of 1935 would demonstrate, the Franklin County sheriff and virtually all of his deputies were deeply involved in the criminal conspiracy. The deputy sheriffs assigned to the Ferrum area under Sheriff Peter Hodges and later his son Sheriff Wilson Hodges during the period 1928 to1935 included Lewis E. Bridges, Luther Smith, Virgil Foster and Howard Maxey. Both Bridges and Smith were fired in February 1929 for refusing to participate in the granny fee conspiracy scheme to protect bootleggers from prosecution in exchange for cash.

Bridges was a primary witness for the prosecution in the 1935 federal trial despite his having been accused previously of arson and prosecuted for the murder of his brother and brother-in-law in 1923. (He was acquitted in that case on the grounds of self-defense.) Maxey was tried as a conspirator in the 1935 trial, but he was one of only three men acquitted by the jury out of more than twenty defendants.

Little wonder then that the law-abiding citizens would seek to have a peace officer who was not associated with a corrupt sheriff's office. Mr. Foster was appointed by the judge and did serve the community as a county policeman. He was succeeded by Taylor Allman. With the convictions in the 1935 trial, the corruption within the sheriff's office was largely erased. The need of the village for its own police officer ended completely when the fire of 1940 destroyed most of Ferrum.

The types of unlawful behavior that prompted some of the residents of the village to petition for a peace officer no doubt consisted primarily of alcohol-related offenses: drunk in public, drunk driving, selling or hauling liquor, disorderly conduct, fighting, and domestic disputes. More serious crimes including arson, robbery and murder did occur.

In June of 1923 near the Ferrum Post Office, a drunken man shot and killed John Robert Buckner, Sr. Buckner, a local mail carrier and a well-respected family man, left behind a wife and four children. The murderer was convicted, given a long prison sentence, and banned for life from Franklin County. In the 1940's, a member of a very prominent local family set fire to two houses in the village. He spent the remainder of his life in an insane asylum.

In the late 1950's, robbers successfully held up The First National Bank of Ferrum and escaped, but not before the diminutive bank cashier C.L. Ross, a WWI veteran, fired a few shots at their speeding get-away car--or so the story goes. In the 1970's, when drug users became more desperate and daring, they resorted to robbing and burglarizing drug stores. Green's Pharmacy experienced both with the night time burglary attempt ending in gun fire. Hugh Green, his son Ricky, and father-in-law Claire Young armed themselves and went to the drugstore when the night alarm sounded. When Green confronted one of the burglars, the man fired a small caliber pistol and wounded Green in the arm before making his escape. A second burglar was apprehended in the pharmacy.

If law and order were problematic in the twentieth century as they clearly were, the preceding eras must have been even more so. Law and order on the frontier would doubtlessly have been largely a might makes right proposition. Settlers would resolve personal and property disputes as best they could. Courts were few, distant, and ever changing as the land that became Franklin County was in whole or in part between 1634 and 1786 assigned to at least eight antecedent counties including Charles City, Prince George, Brunswick, Lunenburg, Bedford, Halifax, Pittsylvania, and Henry. All would have had a court with jurisdiction over the land that would eventually become Franklin County.

The first court to sit in Franklin County did so on January 2, 1786, in the Washington Iron Works ironmaster's house which still stands in Rocky Mount (The home of Dr. J. Francis Amos and Laquita Ramsey Amos). The first sheriff in the new county was Robert Woods, one of the original twelve gentlemen justices. He owned land near what is now Ferrum in the southwestern portion of the county that had been part of Henry County where he had also served as a justice. Prior to the final ratification of the U.S. Constitution in March 1789 and the abolition of cruel and unusual punishment (Amendment VIII), colonial justice could be, and often was, both cruel and unusual.

On September 13, 1786, Sheriff Woods led to the bar of justice one Robert Edmonds who was accused of stealing a squirrel skin purse containing a small amount of money. Upon finding Edmonds guilty, the Franklin County Justices sentenced him "to stand one half hour in the pillory, to receive thirty-nine lashes on his bare back and have both ears cropped" (Greer, *Genesis* 112). Sheriff Woods would have been responsible for seeing the order of the court executed. The extended Woods family of Ferrum traces their lineage from Robert Woods, first sheriff of Franklin County and a Revolutionary War veteran.

Chapter 15

Number, Please

Arguably the railroad connected Ferrum and all of southwestern Franklin County to the rest of the world by simply making it possible for ordinary folks to travel out of the mountains and for news, merchandise, and people to make their way into the mountains. In addition, modern communication in the form of the telegraph arrived with the railroad. Telegraph poles and lines are clearly visible along the tracks in all of the early photographs of the train tracks. Station masters had to learn Morse code and pass on information to train crews often by means of a wooden hoop with the message attached.

The telegraph was followed not long after by the telephone. The Mutual Telephone Exchange of Ferrum was in operation by 1912 with connection to the exchange in Rocky Mount (Merritt 130). In 1921, the company officers were J.W. Wade (1860-1941) of Nola, President; and T.D. McGhee, Vice-president; Milton L. Goode (1880-1963), Secretary, both of Ferrum (L. Stanley, 2014 11). Rates (called dues) at that time amounted to about six dollars per year (L. Stanley, 2014 11). The *Spring 1924 Telephone Directory* for the Franklin County Telephone Company which included the Ferrum Mutual Telephone Company lists 261 subscribers in the Ferrum area. This same directory contained specific directions for properly answering a telephone call:

When answering calls do not say 'hello,' but announce your

name. By observing the above rule much time may be saved, as in nearly every case when the called party answers 'hello' the calling party asks 'who is this?' Whereas, if the name had been given instead of 'hello' the conversation would go ahead immediately.

Clearly, this "rule" did not catch on with the public.

A 1928 telephone book shows how strict the phone company (by this time the Lee Telephone Company) attempted to be in controlling who could use a subscriber's telephone; if anyone outside the subscriber's immediate family or not in his employ made a call, then the subscriber was required to collect a fee from the unauthorized user and submit the fee to the company (L. Stanley, 2015 2).

Before the introduction of automatic switching equipment, an operator had to maintain the switchboard to direct calls. More often than

Figure 1.   An early twentieth century photo of a young woman operating a telephone exchange switchboard in a private home. (State Historical Society of North Dakota)

not, these switchboards were located in people's homes so that calls could be directed anytime day or night. Young women in the community were sometimes hired to operate the switchboard. As late as the 1930's they were paid $15.00 per month and provided room and board (*Callaway of Yesterday* 60). William F. Buckley once observed, perhaps accurately, that had not automated telephone switching devices been invented, every woman in America would have to be employed as a switchboard operator by the phone companies to handle the volume of calls today.

In 1940, the Ferrum switchboard was located in the Hurt Building and was one of the first casualties of the disastrous 1940 fire. All communication to Rocky Mount and the only county fire department was lost, delaying any help from that source until the conflagration was beyond control. Phone service improved markedly after WWII, but party lines were common with numerous houses having to share the telephone line with their neighbors. Needless to say, phone privacy was non-existent until the 1960's and the coming of universal private lines.

Electrical service was introduced in Franklin County in the early 1900's when the Rocky Mount Power Company generated electricity from a hydroelectric power dam on Pigg River primarily to power the newly-formed Bald Knob Furniture Factory. Appalachian Power Company in Roanoke bought this company in 1926 and began to extend electrical service beyond Rocky Mount (Salmon 453). The Ferrum

Figure 2.   Before the introduction of electricty, the oil lamp was a principal source of lighting. (Courtesy of the Blue Ridge Institute)

165

businesses had electricity after WWI. The power came from Fieldale in Henry County where the emerging furniture factories there no doubt gained quicker access to electricity, and Ferrum was close enough to benefit. There is evidence that the new public elementary school built in 1928 had electricity.

The location of Ferrum Training school and the influence of Dr. Benjamin Beckham (1868-1957) also could have expedited the arrival in 1931 of electric power to the area near the village while large parts of the county would not have electricity until after the end of WWII. Prior to rural electrification the Training School produced its own power and light with a steam turbine system located on campus (Hurt, *History* 57). In a 1915 promotional advertisement for Ferrum Training School, Dr. Beckham cites among the school's amenities, "Hot and cold running water, steam heat, and electric lights throughout all buildings" (Hurt, *History* 62). Before the advent of electricity, the homes and businesses of the village would have been lit by kerosene lamps or carbide gas systems and later Delco battery storage systems. Some larger enterprises such as the Algoma orchards, packing houses and canneries at Callaway also generated their own electricity (Salmon 372).

Chapter 16

The Builder Extraordinaire

A few of the family homes of some of the more prominent Ferrum merchants and professionals have been mentioned in passing. Another group of dwellings merits comment because of the man who designed and built them in the 1920's and 1930's. A direct descendant of one of the earliest families who settled along the headwaters of Story Creek, William C. (Billy) Pinckard (1886-1940) was a remarkable self-taught architect and builder. Diane Pendergast in a 1995 article in *Blue Ridge Traditions* credits Pinckard with building no fewer than eight houses in Ferrum and an unknown number around the village. He also built houses and commercial buildings in West Virginia, Tennessee, and New York.

Dwellings in Ferrum built by Pinckard include the Guy and Helen Nolen house (1935), now owned by Donald and Kathy Dodson; the Dr. G. W. Boothe house now owned by Larry Bowling; the Dr. J.M. and Lola Maxey Green house (1940), now owned by Dr. Walter Green; the William Ross house, now owned by Mark and Laura Henne ; the Jack and Blanche Menefee house (1936), now owned by Randell Edwards; the C.L. and Kate Ross house (1924), now owned by Robert and Barbara Ross; the Judson and Clyde Hickman Mullins house, now owned by Hugh Brewer; the Billy and Beulah Menefee Pinckard house, now owned by Marsha Stanley Fay; the C.A. and Berta Turner Hickman house, now owned by Terry and Caitlin Dameron. The last three of these houses

169

Figure 1.   Robert Martin,
Buford Nolen, and Billy Pinckard
are pictured here in the early 1920's.
(Courtesy of the Franklin County
Historical Society)

were fully and beautifully restored over the course of several years beginning in the 1980's by James and Polly Stanley and their daughter Marsha Stanley Fay.

Hallmarks of Pinckard houses included interior arches, French doors, built-in glass-fronted book cases, and distinctive brickwork on the fireplaces and on the exterior, decorative columns and corbels. He also often included separate one-room guest quarters. In the case of the 1936 Jack Menefee house, the guest room was

Figure 2.   Billy Pinckard standing in the main street of Ferrum
circa 1930. (Courtesy of the Blue Ridge Institute)

Figure 3.   The Guy and Helen Nolen house was designed and built by Pinckard in 1935. (Courtesy of the Blue Ridge Institute)

Figure 4.   The Will Ross house was built by Pinckard. (Courtesy of the Blue Ridge Institute)

attached to the main house by a covered carport and had running water and a small wood stove for heat. The Menefees evidently had a live-in maid who used this "guest" room. Of course, the amusing irony is that the house did not have an indoor toilet when it was first built! People had their priorities even in those days apparently.

Pendergast writes in the article that Pinckard's contemporaries considered him a genius because of his originality, his ingenuity, his mastery of mathematics and geometry, and his unfailing attention to detail. It should be noted that Pinckard was ably assisted by local carpenters and craftsmen like Robert Martin (1887-1976). She concludes her tribute to Pinckard, "If we admit to have any appreciation for quality, style, grace, elegance, or craftsmanship, as it pertains to period architecture, then certainly we should pay tribute to Billy Pinckard, the 'builder extraordinaire' (Pendergast 1,3,4).

Figure 5.   The Jack and Blanche Menefee house was built by Pinckard in 1936. (Courtesy of the Blue Ridge Institute)

Figure 6.   The Judson and Clyde Hickman Mullins house was built by Pinckard on Flint Hill. (Courtesy of the Blue Ridge Institute)

Figure 7.   Billy Pinckard built and shared this house with his wife Beulah Menefee Pinckard on Flint Hill. (Courtesy of the Blue Ridge Institute)

Figure 8. *The C.A. and Berta Turner Hickman house was built by Pinckard in 1924 next door to his own home. (Courtesy of the Blue Ridge Institute)*

Chapter 17

Simple Gifts

To conclude this brief history of Ferrum, a few words should be devoted to the ways people of all times and places find to enjoy the simple gifts and pleasures of life. How the people of the village have entertained themselves has changed markedly over the years. Today with access to cable and satellite television, the internet, and a myriad of social media, people hardly need leave their living rooms to have an almost unlimited supply of distractions. Obviously, this was not always the case.

Even before the turn of the twentieth century, however, a surprising number of periodicals were available by mail for the literate in and around Ferrum. Pedro Slone in his 1943 memoir, *The Way of Life in Turner's Creek Valley Sixty Years Ago* lists some of the magazines he remembered reading in his youth. Slone who has been quoted often in this history was a teacher, a mail carrier, an amateur historian, a naturalist, a photographer and a chronicler. He remembers fondly reading from such publications as *Comfort, Good Stories, Yankee Blade, Farm Journal, Saturday Blade, Chicago Ledger,* and *Barkers Comic Almanac.* He mentions too that the first mail-order catalog with its undoubtedly fascinating array of goods came from Lynn and Company of New York. Readers in the community could choose from three weekly newspapers, the *Lynchburg News* as well as the Floyd and Franklin weeklies. Big Lick (Roanoke) and Danville had newspapers that began publishing in the nineteenth century, but Slone

Figure 1. *Between 1920 and 1950 the radio was a primary source of in-home entertainment. (Courtesy of the Library of Congress)*

mentions neither in his memoir (P. Slone, Memoir 19).

From the nineteen-teens and twenties people of means purchased hand-wound Victrolas and recordings as well as player pianos and other musical instruments. (In 1909 one household out of 100 had a piano.) Those with electricity or battery powered systems purchased radio sets and for the first time had real-time access to the outside world and could listen to the current news or music with the turn of a knob.

By the 1930's, motion pictures were available in the larger towns and cities if one had the money and transportation to get there. The heyday for the movies was the 1940's when the main roads were paved, jobs and money were more plentiful, and there was no competition from television. The 1950's saw the arrival of television with its almost mesmerizing hold on people. Every night of the week offered westerns, crime shows, situation comedies, musical variety shows, quiz shows and a goodly number of old movies thrown in for good measure.

Before radios, movies and televisions, folks could be relied upon to create their own forms of entertainment. In fact, almost any excuse would do to gather people together for fun and good times. Fun and work were often combined in corn shucking, quilting bees, molasses boiling, apple butter making, or in most any enterprise where "many hands made light work." When the work was done, the fun began. Out would come local musicians with their fiddles, banjos, guitars and mandolins; making music as they called it seemed to be an inheritable talent in some families. Cloggers and flatfooters would crowd the dance floor carrying on a dance tradition little changed from that brought to the new world by their Scots-Irish ancestors. Drinking and gambling on anything from foot races to horse races to shooting contests to horseshoe pitching only added to the general merriment.

Local musicians who were active from the 1920's to the 1950's and

Figure 2.   Ferrum musicians Walter (Peg) Hatcher, Raymond Slone, and Archie Ross are shown here in the 1950's. (Courtesy of the Blue Ridge Institute)

were often praised for their talent include Archie Ross, Raymond Slone, Jim Mullins, Howard Maxey, Dr. William Lloyd, Walter Edwards, Walter (Peg) Hatcher, and Ted Boyd. Several of these fellows formed the Ferrum

Figure 3. Balloon ascensions along with circuses and medicine shows were much anticipated entertainments. These events were often staged in the open area near the Ike Ferguson House a few hundred yards west of the railroad station. (Courtesy of the Blue Ridge Institute)

String Band and played for ice cream suppers and many other local gatherings. Maxey and Lloyd made at least one recording. Celebrated Old-Time musicians like Charlie Poole and Lonnie Austin often visited Ferrum for the music and the strong drink. Musicians like Monroe Boyd, Edward Montgomery, Cordell Pinckard, Gene Parker, Roger Handy, Carl Scott, Junior Sisk and Billy Boyd among others have carried on the musical traditions passed down to them by their forebears.

Christmas was largely a church and family affair, but at the end of the season something called "Breaking up Christmas" occurred. In some homes furniture was moved aside, rugs and carpets were rolled up, the musicians were invited in and everyone ushered out the holiday by dancing the night away. Such a celebration seems an appropriate way to bid farewell to the old year and welcome in the new one.

Clearly these people could entertain themselves, but they welcomed outside sources of amusement whenever they were in the offing. Pedro Slone in his 1955 monograph on early Ferrum offers a colorful description of the traveling shows that came to the village in its first decades.

> A half-century ago the young people of Ferrum and vicinity looked forward to the coming of the traveling circus. Occasionally it arrived in the springtime, but usually it pitched its tents in the autumn on the bottom land a few hundred yards northwest of the railroad station. The older folk and children alike greatly enjoyed this entertainment. Sometimes we were treated to a never-to-be forgotten balloon ascension. People came from long distances to attend these shows. Another attraction was the traveling medicine man who brought along his numerous bottles and performed his magic tricks. The writer recalls one such person by the name of Sans Blas, whose eloquence equaled, if not surpassed, that of Daniel Webster or William Jennings Bryan. He always made a speech after which he held a bottle and made his lusty call, 'Gentleman over here gets one!' pointing in a certain direction. The bystander could not resist his urging and would invest the price of two hundred pounds of tan-bark or a couple of cross ties for a bottle of 'cureall,' which he probably never took, or never even carried home after he came out from under the hypnotic spell. (P. Slone, *History* 9)

To be continued…

Afterword

It is only fitting that Mr. Slone should have had the last word, and a happy one at that, for he, more than anyone else, is responsible for this latest installment in the history of Ferrum. In a few years, perhaps someone else with an interest in local history will pick up the story and continue the tradition that he began in 1955 with what he called his "historical sketch of Ferrum, Virginia." I owe him a debt of gratitude. Other local amateur historians and genealogists come to mind as well: Max Thomas, Frank Hurt, Raymond Slone, Mabel France, Edith Sigmon, Gladys Edwards Willis, Sarah Quinn, Hazel Via Hale, James Stanley, and more recently Becky Cannaday Merchant, Shirley Hale Whitlow, Beverly Merritt, Morris Stephenson, and Lane Hash.

Undertaking a research project, even as limited in scale as this one, brings much joy and much frustration. Joy in discovering information in plain sight or tucked away and almost forgotten, and joy in meeting and talking with folks of all ages who were willing to share their memories and knowledge.

The greatest frustration undoubtedly came in the realization that I had waited too late to begin this research. Of course, many who had firsthand knowledge of early Ferrum were long dead, but even as I began this research I lost folks like Col. James Stanley, Dexter Mullins, and C.B. Nolen, Jr. who possessed a wealth of knowledge about the village that I barely began to plumb.

Frustrating, too, has been my inability to flesh out what would have been fascinating stories such as the "witch of Ferrum" who may have been one Duck Moore. Mrs. Moore was accused of casting evil spells on her neighbors only to have her husband, Montague Moore, later appear and offer to remove the spell in exchange for food or cash (R. Slone 18). In our more modern, less superstitious times, these two folks sound more like shakedown artists than witches. Another story that I could not substantiate concerned the "Great Circus Train Catastrophe" that is supposed to have occurred in Ferrum when a circus train headed south for the winter got caught in an early snow storm. Tantalizing too, are stories of political bribery and corruption, and yes, even some murder mysteries that remain to be solved.

I will apologize in advance for both minor and major mistakes in the text. I have tried to be as accurate as I could be with names, spellings, dates, events, place names, and other facts knowing full well I was bound to fall short. Any sins of omission or commission are regretted.

This brief history ends with the notation "To be continued…" for two reasons. The first reason is that I know that I have found only a sampling of what is out there: photographs, letters, diaries, memories. In the hope that others will come forward with information that will add to this history, I am providing the proceeds from the sale of this book and a modest endowment to the Blue Ridge Institute of Ferrum College for the purpose of collecting and archiving information, pictures, and artifacts related to the history of the village of Ferrum, Virginia. The second is simple: Ferrum lives on, and the present and even the future will be soon enough the stuff of history.

In 2019, a group of citizens interested in the future of Ferrum organized a civic group to enhance the quality of life in the Ferrum community. Building upon on a multi-year county study of the needs of the community, this group calling itself Ferrum Forward has begun identifying community improvement priorities and making concrete plans to implement the improvements.

Karl L. Edwards

edkwards@embarqmail.com

October 2019

Appendix

Landscape Views of Ferrum: Then and Now

Figure 1.   This photo taken from Menefee Hill looks west towards Ferrum College in about 1930. The unpaved Route 40 appears on the left-hand side. To the right of Route 40 in the near foreground is the low-lying area that was used as the showgrounds for circuses and medicine shows at the turn of the twentieth century. (Courtesy of the Blue Ridge Institute)

Figure 2.   This photo taken in 2019 from Menefee Hill looks to the west toward Ferrum College. Jamison's Knob appears in the distance on the left and Saul's Knob (Ferrum Mountain) appears in the distance on the right.
(Courtesy of the Blue Ridge Institute)

Figure 3. This photo taken in the mid-1920's looks southwest over the village of Ferrum. The railroad station appears in the right foreground. The Ferrum Bank and J.K. Hurt and Company appear in the center of the photo. (Courtesy of the Blue Ridge Institute)

Figure 4.   This photo taken in 2019 shows the main street of Ferrum with the Thompson Building in the right foreground. Heavy equipment sits on the site of the railroad station just left of center. (Courtesy of the Blue Ridge Institute)

Figure 5. This photo taken circa 1937 looking north shows the main street of Ferrum. On the extreme left this photograph affords a rare glimpse of the first brick Menefee Building . (Courtesy of the Blue Ridge Institute)

Figure 6.   This photograph taken in 2019 looks down the main street of Ferrum toward the north with Saul's Knob in the distance. (Courtesy of the Blue Ridge Institute)

Works Cited

"Accent on People – Dr. J.M. Green." *Martinsville Bulletin*, 14 July 1974, p. 1E.

Bowling, Larry. Personal interview. 28 May 2015.

Cemetery Records of Franklin County, Virginia. Baltimore, Maryland: Gateway Press, Inc., 1986.

Claiborne, J.G.: *Franklin County Virginia-Historical and Industrial Past, Present, and Future*. Lynchburg, Virginia. 1926.

Cobbs, Cabell F. "Doc." *The Mountain Laurel: The Journal of Mountain Life*. August, 1987.

"County Utilities." Franklin County Virginia, http://www.franklincountyva.gov/utilities.

Crowder, Chris. "Roanoke and Southern Railway." *Avalon: Documenting the Rise and Fall of a Cotton Mill Village*, 2019, www.avalonmills.com/story3.php.

Cundiff, Dorothy R., editor. *Yesterday and Today*. Vol. 22, Collinsville Printing Co., 1993.

Drewery, S. R. *Yesterday and Today* Vol. 7, Rocky Mount, Virginia: Franklin County Retail Merchants Association.

Franklin County Cemeteries. Rocky Mount, Virginia: Franklin County Historical Society, 1997.

Franklin County Post Offices Over the Years. Rocky Mount, Virginia: Franklin County Historical Society, 2005.

Gearhart, James. Personal interview. 2015.

Greer, T. Keister. *Genesis of a Virginia Frontier: The Origins of Franklin County, Virginia 1740-1785*. Rocky Mount, Virginia: History Home Press, 2005.

---. *The Great Moonshine Conspiracy Trial of 1935*. Rocky Mount, Virginia: History House Press, 2002.

Goode, Edward. E-mail to Lee Cheatham, 6 October 2014.

Goode, Kyle Edward. Telephone interview. 1 June, 2015.

---. Personal interview. 9 May 2017.

Green, Hugh. Personal interview. 2018.

Green, Shirley Young. Telephone interview. 1 June 2015.

Hartley, T.A. "A Look Back" (Franklin County Public Schools). Rocky Mount, Virginia: *Franklin County High School Yearbook-The Animo, 1986*.

Hash, John and Mary Boone Hash. *Calendar of Events 1909-1959 of James Goode Hash*. Nashville, TN: Printing Etc., 1997.

Hudson, Tipton. Interview. *Yesterday and Today*. Vol. 22. Rocky Mount, Virginia: Franklin County Retail Merchants Association, 1993.

Hurt, Frank Benjamin. *A History of Ferrum College*. Roanoke, Virginia: Stone Printing Company, 1977.

---. "Reflections on the Origin of Ferrum College." *Bicentennial Reflections; County of Franklin-Virginia 1786-1986*. Rocky Mount, Virginia: Franklin County Bicentennial Commission, 1986.

Meador, Jean Ingram. Telephone interview. 28 May 2015.

Merchant, Becky Cannaday. *Over in the Country: a Blue Ridge Mountain Family's Stories*. Buena Vista, Virginia: Mariner Publishing, 2008.

Merritt, Beverly, ed. *Marshall Wingfield's History of Franklin County, Virginia*. Rocky Mount, Virginia: Computer Shock, 2015.

Mills, Frank. "Stave Mills and Cooper Shops". *Callaway of Yesterday*. Callaway, Virginia: Green Thumb Garden Club, 2005.

Mullins, Dexter. Telephone interview. 2015.

Mullins, Harold. Telephone interview. 2018.

Pendergast, Diana. "He Left a Thumbprint of Excellence." *Rocky Mount, Virginia: Blue Ridge Traditions*, Vol. 3, No. 2, September, 1995.

Ramsey, Harold W. "Personal Reflections of Harold W. Ramsey". Rocky Mount, Virginia: Franklin County Historical Society, 2006.

---. "Profiles of Teachers I Have Known." Rocky Mount, Virginia: 1972.

Robertson, Lizzie Cole. "Callaway Public Schools." *Callaway of Yesterday*. Callaway, Virginia: Green Thumb Garden Club, 2005.

Rocky Mount, Virginia Railroadin' Since 1880. Rocky Mount, Virginia: Franklin County Historical Publications, 2000.

Salmon, John. S and Emily J. Salmon. *Franklin County Virginia 1786-1986 A Bicentennial History*. Rocky Mount, Virginia: Franklin County Bicentennial Commission, 1993.

"Schools: Teacher Contract." (Laura Montgomery-1905), *Callaway of Yesterday*. Callaway, Virginia: Green Thumb Garden Club, 2005.

Slone, Pedro T. Memoir, February 1943. "The Way of Life in Turner's Creek Valley Sixty Years Ago." Blacksburg, Virginia: Special Collections, Virginia Polytechnic Institute and State University.

---. Monograph: "Historical Sketch of Ferrum, Virginia.":Henry County Historical Society, 1955.

Slone, Raymond. *Uncle Esom's Grist Mill – other stories, folktales & tall tales*. c. 1981.

Smith, Essie Wade. "History of Franklin County-Unfinished Manuscript". Rocky Mount, Virginia: Franklin County Bicentennial Commission, 1977.

Stanley, Lt. Col. James. Personal interview. 21 September, 2015.

---. "Saint James Methodist Church 1896-1996." Ferrum, Virginia: 1997.

Stanley, Linda, ed. *The Times of Franklin*. Rocky Mount, Virginia: Franklin County Historical Society, June, 2014.

---. *The Times of Franklin*. Rocky Mount, Virginia: Franklin County Historical Society, April, 2015.

Stephenson, Morris, Merritt, Beverly, Leary, Angie. *Franklin County's Famous 1935 Moonshine Conspiracy Trial: Complete Daily Newspaper Accounts*. Rocky Mount, Virginia, 2016.

Swartz, William P. "Early Virginia Railroads." *The Mountain Laurel: The Journal of Mountain Life*. September, 1987.

Virginia Department of Transportation. "A History of Roads in Virginia". 2006, virginiadot.org/about/resources/historyofrds.pdf

Webb, James. *Born Fighting: How the Scots-Irish Shaped America.* Broadway Books. New York. 2004,

Webb, Vaughan, ed. *Franklin County Life and Culture: A Pictorial Record.* Ferrum, Virginia: Blue Ridge Institute of Ferrum College, 1986.

Willis, Gladys Edwards, *Goin' Up Shootin' Creek.* History,Etc., Inc.

Wingfield, Marshall. *Franklin County Virginia: A History.* Berryville, Virginia: Chesapeake Book Company, 1964.

Wright, Elvie Kesler. "The First Church of the Brethern of Ferrum." circa 1989.

Young, Cecil. Personal interview. 2017.

Index

Fuson, John 5

G

Garst, Jack 21
Gaubatz Painting Company 145
George A. Menefee 67
Gillispie, Jacqueline 56
Gillispie, Roger 56
Goode, Edward 64, 105, 125
Goode, Emma 75
Goode Family 13
    Brothers 33
Goode, George C. 45
Goode, George E. 48, 69, 77
Goode, Kyle 64
Goode, Milton L 163
Goode, Mrs. Minnie 75
Goode, Virgil H., Jr. 114
Goodpasture, M.G. 78
Gravely, Anne Carter Lee 6
Great Depression 31, 143
Great Wagon Road 5
Great Warriors Path 1
Great Warriors Trace 1, 5
Green, Darnell Young 73
Green, Dr. John Monroe 32, 55, 57, 58, 59, 60, 64, 69, 90, 157, 158, 169
Green, Dr. Walter 169
Green, Hugh 37, 61, 160
Green, Lola Maxey 169
Green, Ricky 149, 160
Green, Shirley Young 37, 61, 85
Green's Pharmacy 37, 38, 61, 160
Greer, Keister 2
Guerrant, S.S. 21, 25
Guilliams, Edgecomb 3

H

Hairston, Dr. William 55
Hale, Des 105
Hale, Eddie 149
Hale, Giles W.B. 19
Halifax County 160
Handy, Donald 105
Handy, Roger 180
Hanes, H.W. 117
Hardie, L.H. 55
Harrison, Katrina 146
Hash, W.P. 77
Hawpatch Road 70
Haynes, Brooks 46, 89
Haynes Family 5
Haynes, John W. 69
Haynes' Knob 9
Haynes, Marshall 46
H.E. Menefee and Company:
General Merchandise 23
Henne, Laura 169
Henne, Mark 169
Henry 81
    High School 80
Henry County 105, 117, 140, 143, 152, 160, 166
Henry Road 70
Hickman and Menefee store 98
Hickman, Berta Turner 169, 174
Hickman Building 90
Hickman, Charles A. 33, 34, 49, 70, 77, 89, 157, 169, 174
    Hickman General Merchandise Store 89
Hickman Family 13
Hidden Treasures 145, 146
Hill, Robert 3
Hill, Swinfield 63

128, 130, 170
Stanley Furniture 143
Stanley, Polly 170
Stanley, T.A. 143
Stanley, Thomas B. 143
Stanley, Winfred E. 37, 148
Starry Creek 9
Stevens, Ron 105
Stock Market Crash 30
Stone, Ben 60
Story Creek 5, 20, 63, 64, 69, 108, 142, 169
Strouth, Garlin 53
Stuart 148
Summit Cut 11, 98, 117
Summit Hill 63
Supreme Court Brown v. Board of Education 84
Swartz, William P. 124
Swietzer, Rev. William 52

T

Tatum, Tim 86
Terry, P.L. 117
Thompson, Bertha 70
Thompson, Bobby 86
Thompson Building 32, 37
Thompson, Harvey 146
Thompson Ridge Road 53, 70
Thompson, W. Bunyan 28, 31, 32, 38
Thornton Mountain 69
Thornton, William L. 33, 34, 45
Timber Line Road 14, 38, 106, 149
Town Creek 1
Tri-Area Community Health Clinic 51, 57

Trout, H.S. 117
Turner 13, 14
Turner, Ben 14
Turner, Berta 34
Turner, F.F. 77, 158
Turner, G.A. 157
Turner, George A. 20, 67, 69
Turner, Henry M. 33, 34
Turner, Robert 3
Turners Creek 1
Turner's Creek Road 67, 83
Turner, Sophronia Luke 67
Tutelo 1

U

Underwood, Wiley 143
U.S. Constitution 160
U.S. Public Law 94-142, the Education of All Handicapped Children Act 85

V

Vaughn, Dr. John 57
Vernon, J.A. 60
Victrolas 178
Virginia Apparel Company 145
Virginia Department of Education 75
Virginia Department of Transportation 107
Virginia General Assembly 117, 152
Virginia Highway Commissioner 114
Virginia House of Burgesses 3
Virginia Mills Corporation (Silk Mill) 144
V-J Day 63

W

Wade Family 13, 14
Wade, J.W. 85, 163
Wade, Mattie 75
Wade, Sim 38
Wagoner, Charles 105
Waidsboro 70, 108, 136
Waidsboro Road 70
Waid Stagecoach Stop 9
Walker, T.A. 75
Ward Family 13
Ward, Jennie 12
Ward, Julia 78
Ward, Samuel 12, 78
Ward, Sarah Elizabeth 12
Warwick Road 5
Washington Iron Works 63, 160
Weaver, R.E. 143
Webb, J. V. 143
Webster, Daniel 181
W. Hank Norton Highway 114
Whippet automobiles 148
Whitehead, Mary Hurt 32, 33, 60, 93
Whitehead, R.E. 158
Whitlock, Cleonard 105
Whittaker, Era 62
Wieble, Dr. Donald 57
William L. Thornton 33, 45, 69
Williams, Dr. J. M. 45, 55
Willis, Gladys Edwards 22, 56, 62, 120, 124, 128
Wilson, Phillip 114
Wingfield, Marshall 32, 33, 62, 132
Wirtz 11, 136
Women's Missionary Society 77
Woodcott Road 52, 146

Wood Family 13
Woods, J.R.L. 77
Woods, Richard 70
Woods, Robert 160, 161
Woods, Ronnie 86
Woods, Wilbur 36
World War I 137, 142, 166
World War II 63, 130, 165, 166
Worley, Ruby Woods 98, 128

Y

Young 13, 14
Young, Elma Scott 32, 73
Young, E.M. 77
Young, George Claire 32, 33, 37, 73, 85, 103, 108, 144, 147, 148, 149, 160
Young, G.W. 19
Young, Jehu 12
Young, Keiko 62
Young, Lewis 12
Young, Oliver 157
Young, Peter 11
Young, R.H. 89
Young, Robert 12, 62
Young's Garage 93, 148
Young's Hardware and Grocery 33

About the Author

Karl L. Edwards grew up in Ferrrum and attended the local public school through the ninth grade. He graduated from Franklin County High School in 1963. From 1963 to 1967 he attended the College of William and Mary and graduated with a Bachelor's degree in English. He earned a Master of Arts in Liberal Studies degree from Hollins University in 1977. In addition, he completed further graduate studies at William and Mary, VPI&SU, and the University of Virginia. From 1968 to 2000 he worked in the public schools of Franklin County and retired in 2000 as Associate Principal of Franklin County High School.

Made in the USA
Monee, IL
08 February 2020